KANSAS CITY

...and All That's

JAZZ

KANSAS CITY

The Kansas City Jazz Museum

. . . and All That's JAZZ

SICIANS ASSN. BLDG
LOCAL NO. 627
CIAN FEDERATION of MUSICIANS

PAUL BANKS

May 4, 1930

J. E. Miller Studio

A DONNA MARTIN BOOK

Andrews McMeel Publishing

Kansas City

www.andrewsmcmeel.com

Library of Congress Cataloging-in-Publication Data

Kansas City— and all that's jazz / the Kansas City Jazz Museum.
    p.   cm.
    Published in conjunction with the new museum's first exhibition.
    "A Donna Martin book."
    Includes discography, bibliographical references, and videography.
    ISBN 0-8362-6829-6 (hardcover). — ISBN 0-8362-6828-8 (pbk.)
    1. Jazz—Missouri—Kansas City—Exhibitions. 2. Kansas City
Jazz Museum—Exhibitions. I. Kansas City Jazz Museum.
    ML141.K3K365   1999
    781.65'074'778411—dc21   98-34242
                                                                     CIP
                                                                     MN

Credits for cover photos:
Top row, left to right: Mary Lou Williams, The *Kansas City Call*; Charlie Parker, *Schomburg Center for Research in Black Culture*; Duke Ellington, *Kansas City Jazz Museum, VeEssa Spivey Collection*; Count Basie, *Kansas City Jazz Museum, VeEssa Spivey Collection*; Jay McShann, *Kansas City Jazz Museum, John Baker Collection*; Ella Fitzgerald, *Kansas City Jazz Museum, John Baker Collection*. Center: George E. Lee's Singing Novelty Orchestra, *Kansas City Museum, Goin' To Kansas City Collection, Charles Goodwin*. Bottom row, left to right: Myra Taylor, The *Kansas City Call*; Oran "Hot Lips" Page, *The Kansas City Call*; Louis Armstrong, *Kansas City Jazz Museum, Goin' To Kansas City Collection, Arthur McClure and Jennie Belle Peters*; Julia Lee, The *Kansas City Call*; Lester Young, The *Kansas City Call* ; Big Joe Turner, *Kansas City Jazz Museum, John Baker Collection*.

ATTENTION: SCHOOLS AND BUSINESSES

Andrews McMeel books are available at quantity discounts with bulk purchase for educational, business, or sales promotional use. For information, please write to: Special Sales Department, Andrews McMeel Publishing, 4520 Main Street, Kansas City, Missouri 64111.

CONTENTS

JAZZ FOREWORD

JAZZ IS—exciting, exhilarating, subtle, profound, raw, vital, vast, emotional, an unbelievable high . . . life.

In 1989 the City Council of Kansas City allocated $20 million to rekindle the once-vibrant life of what was one of the most famous jazz districts in America, 18th and Vine. One result of that commitment is the Kansas City Jazz Museum and its 10,200-square-foot exhibition, "Kansas City . . . and All That's Jazz." The Kansas City jazz story is vibrant and ever-present, kept alive by the memories, artifacts, and stories of the people who lived it. The exhibition is our initial offering to provide an appreciation of jazz as an African American–originated music that evolved into one of the world's greatest twentieth-century art forms. This book, *Kansas City . . . and All That's Jazz,* serves as a visual tour of our multi-layered exhibition.

The current stage for the Kansas City music tradition is our own Blue Room. This exhibition nightclub provides visitors with an outstanding opportunity to experience—and reflect on—Kansas City's stable of legendary and present-day artists.

The Memory Wall of great Kansas City musicians offers romanticism, hope, and lasting recollections. The intense mural by artist Michael Massenburg connects Kansas City artists to the world jazz scene. The tables in the club send visitors on their own personal pub crawl, filled as they are with memorabilia, artifacts, and photographs of some of the most famous clubs in Kansas City.

The center of the Blue Room is its living performance space, the stage. It comes alive four nights a week with the exhilarating and exciting sounds of Kansas City's finest jazz artists.

This book also features a unique interview with Kansas City jazz legend Jay "Hootie" McShann. This artist will delight you with his illuminating memories and experiences, told in his own words with the feeling and connection that only he could impart.

Also included is an introduction by our music scholar and exhibit consultant, Leonard Brown; a comprehensive selection from our archival photographic collection; an overview of the club scene by Claude Page; and a discography, a videography, and a bibliography, each specially selected to provide additional insight into the Kansas City jazz legacy.

The Board of Directors of the 18th and Vine Authority and the museum staff are excited about the opportunity to present this book, as well as to acknowledge and thank all the musicians, donors, and contributors. We invite you to treasure it as your personal exhibit.

ROWENA STEWART, D.H.
Executive Director

JAZZ: AN AFRICAN AMERICAN GIFT TO THE NATION AND THE WORLD

by Leonard Brown

INTRODUCTION

IN THESE last days of the twentieth century, we often reflect on those innovations, creations, advances, and inventions of the last hundred years that have had great impact on our daily lives. These include radios, phonographs, telephones, records, cassettes, movies, compact disks, tape recorders, satellites, rockets, television sets, airplanes, automobiles, nuclear weapons, women's rights, the civil rights movement, computers, voting rights, affirmative action, desegregation, and the Internet.

It is important to include music in our reflections, because music is one of our oldest and consistently moving forms of expression. In America, one of this century's most powerful forms of music comes from African American culture. This music is commonly known as jazz. Born out of the post-enslavement experiences of African Americans and rooted in the performance traditions and functions of spirituals, field hollers, work songs, gospel, and the blues, jazz spread outward from black communities until today it is one of the most appealing and influential musics ever, having captured the hearts and souls of listeners and musicians worldwide.

The Kansas City Jazz Museum is the first national institution to celebrate jazz and honor the African American culture and the musicians who created it. Opened in the fall of 1997, the museum has the following goals:

1. To provide a greater awareness of and appreciation for jazz as an African American–originated music that has evolved into one of the greatest twentieth-century art forms.

2. To recognize and commemorate some of the musicians and musical groups that made significant contributions to the evolution of jazz.

3. To provide exposure to the important role of Kansas City in the history of jazz.

4. To present some of the aesthetics of jazz, performance and nonperformance.

This section will introduce the African American legacy of jazz. It provides a brief overview of the evolution of jazz in black American communities, including reasons for its unprecedented appeal, gives some basic performance aesthetics, and explains the role of Kansas City in jazz history.

A BRIEF HISTORY OF JAZZ

Throughout the two hundred and fifty plus years of their enslavement in the Americas, Africans and African Americans consistently used vocal music to express their daily life situations and how they felt about it. The powerful singing so characteristic of spirituals, work songs, and field hollers served many purposes during enslavement, with one of the most important being to express the humanity of the enslaved. Reduced to "nonhumans" by the enslavers, the enslaved Blacks used these vocal-dominant musical forms as a primary means of expressing their sadness, confusion, fears, opinions, strengths, hopes, faith, and desires. Music was a force that provided the strength for them to persevere and survive in these worst of times.

The characteristics of these early musics reflected age-old

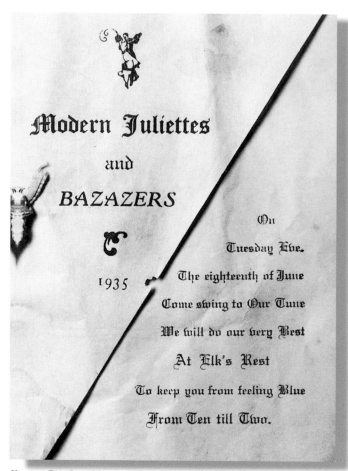

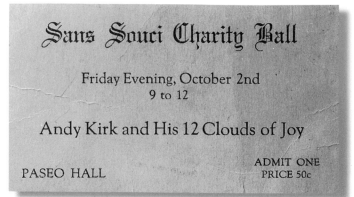

Kansas City Jazz Museum, Irene Marcus Collection

Kansas City Jazz Museum, Irene Marcus Collection

musical traditions that can be found in the various African cultures from which the enslaved were taken. Many of these performance stylizations were maintained and modified during enslavement, including bending and swooping of the voice, call-and-response forms, polyrhythms, strong rhythmic drive, dance, communal participation, and various African concepts of melody and harmony.

After enslavement was ended during the Civil War by the Emancipation Proclamation (1863), African Americans began to have new experiences associated with freedom. Many left the South, spreading north, east, and west in their search for new opportunities. As they created new lives for themselves, they continued to chronicle their experiences in music—particularly in a new style called the blues. This vocal-dominant music used many of the characteristics associated with the African American musics mentioned earlier. Initially, blues was a music created by Blacks for Blacks. But as Blacks gained increased mobility, their music traveled with them and became popular in the dominant culture.

Blues was a music of honesty and sincerity. The sto-

ries told by the words of blues songs expressed many of the daily aspects of life with which the listener could identify. By the end of the nineteenth century, blues were being sung by African American women as part of traveling entertainment shows, which made this music very popular. Known as classic blues singers, such remarkable vocalists as Gertrude "Ma" Rainey, Ida Cox, and Lucille Hegamin spread the blues outside the black community and introduced it to the nation.

At the same time, black musicians began adding various instrumental groups to blues performance. This resulted in increased use of improvisation. Along with blues, ragtime, another black musical genre of the late 1800s, became a favorite among musicians, and they began to expand their musical abilities using the forms and structures of both these musics. By the early 1900s, the term "jazz" was being applied to these new, innovative, and exciting creative performance traditions. African American musicians living in such urban areas as New Orleans, Kansas City, St. Louis, Atlanta, Chicago, Baltimore, and New York continued to develop this new music, creating and pioneering innovative approaches to instrumental performance rooted in the vocal performance traditions of blues and the earlier forms of African American musics.

By the end of the second decade of the twentieth century, jazz had begun to spread around the nation and the world. As African Americans left the South seeking new and better opportunities, they took their music with them, and blues and jazz were heard throughout black communities established in major urban areas of the north, east, and west. During World War I, African Americans, though segregated, were part of the American forces, and James Reese Europe's 369th Band helped introduce jazz to Europeans. Their musical performances left the Europeans spellbound and wanting to hear more of "le jazz hot."

Knock, Knock—Who's There
ACACIA BOYS
SPONSORING
APRON AND OVERALL DANCE
OCTOBER 29TH, 1936
ADMISSION 40c   LABOR TEMPLE

$1.50 Prize—Best dressed man and woman
$1.00 Prize—Tackiest dressed man and woman
IN APRON AND OVERALLS

Kansas City Jazz Museum, Irene Marcus Collection

DANCING
EVERY FRIDAY NIGHT
LINCOLN HALL, 18th & VINE
RYTHM MUSKETEERS
Broadcasting Dance Band
ROSCOE WHITE, Manager
RAY BOOTH
Clubs and Lodges given half of Profits
PASS   ONE

Kansas City Jazz Museum, Irene Marcus Collection

During the 1920s, jazz became the rage of post–World War I America. Known as the Jazz Age, this decade saw jazz gain in popularity both nationally and internationally. Through the innovative and exciting musical styles of such master artists as Louis Armstrong, Ferdinand "Jelly Roll" Morton, Edward Kennedy "Duke" Ellington, Bessie Smith, Fletcher Henderson, Alberta Hunter, Julia and George Lee, Jimmie Lunceford, Bennie Moten, and Earl Hines, jazz became firmly established. These headliners and the many other jazz musicians and singers of the time were pioneers who created the foundations for jazz performance and aesthetics. The invention of the radio and the phonograph helped spread jazz much farther and wider than live performance, increasing exposure to hundreds of thousands and creating a great demand for the new music.

During the 1930s, the jazz style known as swing became very popular. Always linked to dance, jazz was the featured music in many of the large dance halls found in major cities. Much of this jazz maintained a blues flavor. In the Midwest and Southwest, some of the most captivating music came from Kansas City musicians. The bands of Andy Kirk, Bennie Moten, Count Basie, and Jay McShann were known for their use of riffs and vamps and often featured great vocalists such as Jimmy Rushing, Joe Turner, and Pha Terrell. These bands traveled throughout the country, spreading the KC sound nationwide.

Kansas City was a major center for jazz and blues performance because of the large black population there. It was on the regular circuit for dance bands that included Houston, Dallas, and Oklahoma City. In addition, Kansas City was controlled by the Pendergast political machine and was a wide-open town where clubs and dance halls often ran twenty-four hours a day, so there were many opportunities for musicians to play.

Another feature of Kansas City jazz was the jam session. These were informal performances where musicians would gather and play after their regular jobs. Many times there would be "battles" or "cutting sessions" among the performers, with musicians trying to outdo each other. These were not only fun but great learning experiences in which the players shared with and learned from each other.

Kansas City also had what was known as the "Kansas City beat" or "KC swing," characterized by a strong 4/4 rhythm, exciting solos, and the use of riffs. Riffs are short, repeating melodic passages with a strong rhythmic drive. Many credit Bennie Moten with establishing KC swing. Riffs were important in maintaining a functional dance music while providing new opportunities for instrumentalists to develop their improvisational skills.

By the end of the 1930s, swing was *the* popular music in the United States. At the same time, new styles and approaches to jazz performance were being formulated and codified in uptown jam sessions in New York City's Harlem. These approaches were based on a deep understanding of harmonics, increased interplay between the soloist and the rhythm section, longer solos, faster tempos, and virtuoso instrumental performance techniques. Later named "bebop," this style of jazz represented a stage in the continual evolution of the music. Many listeners and musicians were not appreciative of bebop when it came on the scene, primarily because it required a higher level of musical knowledge and technique and began to separate dance from jazz performance. But bebop prevailed and is now recognized as a major step in the evolution of American music. The advanced music created by such great musicians as Dizzy Gillespie, Thelonious Monk, Charlie Christian, Kenny Clarke,

No. 269

CONTEST ENTRIES
Vote For Your Favorite

☒ Coeds
☐ Niftiettes
☐ Duchess
☐ Les Debteins

Deposit this Stub in Ballot
Box at Dance

KANSAS CITY PLAYBOY'S
First Annual
DANCE and POPULARITY CONTEST
Friday, May 14th, 1937 - 9 p. m. Until ?
THE NEWLY DECORATED LINCOLN HALL
18th and Vine

No. 269

Admission 25c in Advance
No Adv. Tickets After May 12th

35c at Door

Kansas City Jazz Museum, Irene Marcus Collection

Max Roach, and Kansas City's own Charlie Parker revolutionized musical concepts. During this time, Afro-Cuban music became linked with bebop, creating the exciting style of musical performance known as cubop.

After World War II, jazz continued to grow and develop. Bebop was the newest style, but all the earlier forms were still being played. By the 1950s, styles known as "cool" and "hard bop" came into being. "Cool" meant a style of jazz that used many of the aesthetic principles of bebop but "cooled down" the strong interplay between the rhythm section and the soloist. The Miles Davis/Gil Evans collaboration *Birth of the Cool* is a classic recording from this period. "Hard bop" was a combination of bebop styles with a more bluesy feel. George Russell's concept of Lydian chromatics set the stage for modal jazz, which has since become a principal performance style. It was in this decade that jazz festivals were born, the first being at Newport, Rhode Island. Since that time, jazz festivals have expanded worldwide. Today, there are more festivals for jazz than for any other type of music.

The 1960s saw jazz performance reflect the social movements for human and civil rights, as African Americans challenged the country to provide the equality for all that was guaranteed in the Constitution. Jazz musicians and their music reflected the same concerns, as illustrated by such titles as "Freedom Suite," "Search for the New Land," "Members Don't Get Weary," "Blacknuss," and "Afrocentric."

There was also a move away from the conventional approaches to jazz performance. Some musicians began to play in ways that were very different from what had been done before. These styles were known as "avant-garde" or "free" jazz and caused a considerable uproar from many listeners and musicians alike. But the musicians persevered, and what was once considered inappropriate is now a part of the jazz legacy. Musical giants such as John Coltrane, Ornette Coleman, Cecil Taylor, and Sun Ra are among those who played outside as well as within the established and accepted jazz traditions. Coltrane, in particular, incorporated a high degree of spirituality into his compositions and performances.

By the 1970s, jazz had become electrified. The introduction of electronic musical instruments led to a new sound and also helped jazz fuse with other popular musical styles, so jazz "fusion" was born. The 1980s and 1990s have seen jazz continue to grow and develop. Having left the African American community and culture that gave it birth and nurtured it to maturity, it is now shared, celebrated, and performed by human beings all over the globe. Jazz-studies programs have become a standard part of many college and university offerings, and the International Association of Jazz Educators is a major organization.

As we move into the twenty-first century, we must remember the basic African American cultural aesthetic on which jazz is built. This aesthetic is rooted in the intent to create music that has a great amount of sincerity and integrity; music that touches people in ways that are meaningful; music that appeals; music that requires one to do one's best and stay open to new approaches. As Edward Kennedy "Duke" Ellington said, "It don't mean a thing if it ain't got that swing."

JAZZ MASTERS

by Leonard Brown

This section presents four of the most outstanding artists in the history of jazz: Louis Armstrong, Duke Ellington, Ella Fitzgerald, and Charlie Parker. These great musicians were chosen because of their outstanding contributions to and achievements in jazz performance, composition, and arranging. Pioneers, creators, and innovators, they changed the face of music forever. Their individual and collective legacies transcend locality and extend worldwide.

LOUIS ARMSTRONG

Trumpet and cornet player, singer, and composer
Born August 4, 1901, in New Orleans, Louisiana
Died July 6, 1971, in Queens, New York

The city where Louis Armstrong was born in 1901 was rich in African American music and culture. An important early center of jazz, New Orleans provided Armstrong many opportunities to hear brass bands, blues singers, gospel choirs, church spirituals, ragtime pianists and bands, and street musicians. He grew up in a turn-of-the-century New Orleans surrounded by the music of its African American community.

Armstrong first learned to play the cornet during the time he lived at the Colored Waifs Home. Early in his career, he was influenced by the music of legendary musicians Joe "King" Oliver, his mentor, and Fate Marable. By the age of seventeen, Armstrong was performing on Mississippi River excursion boats and playing in New Orleans cabarets.

In 1922, Armstrong was called to Chicago to work with King Oliver's Creole Jazz Band. Two years later, he joined Fletcher Henderson's orchestra and moved to New York. During his time with Henderson, Armstrong's spellbinding improvisations expressed deep musical logic and powerful emotion, creating what is known as swing. In 1925, Louis returned to Chicago, where he made the

famous recordings of the Hot Five and Hot Seven bands over the next couple of years.

Armstrong traveled to Europe for the first time in the 1930s and became very popular, with his innovative trumpet playing, scat singing, and engaging personality. Later in the decade he appeared in Hollywood films, which added to his popularity. As one of the first jazz musicians to gain international fame, Armstrong made numerous appearances worldwide over the next thirty years, many for the U.S. State Department. His 1960s recordings of "Hello Dolly" and "Mack the Knife" were big hits.

Using his artistry and creativity, Armstrong expressed deep human values in his music, which listeners throughout the world found irresistible. His musical contributions and his engaging public personality were essential to the spreading of jazz worldwide. He came to symbolize American vitality and paved the way for future jazz stars to be recognized.

As the first great jazz soloist, Armstrong created music that made sense and expressed intelligence and emotion. Rooted in the spirituals and blues of African American culture, Armstrong used his artistry to create an authentic American music that expressed African American feelings and thoughts. His instrumental virtuosity and stylistic innovations led the way for future jazz musicians.

The magnitude of Louis Armstrong's musical contri-

K NOWN the world over as Ambassador Satch and lovingly called Pops by fellow musicians, Louis Armstrong was one of the first great jazz creators and innovators. His fabulous technique on trumpet and cornet enabled him to play unbelievably high notes at incredible speeds. His tone was warm and pure. He was an imaginative improvisational genius and could swing like no one else. His unique vocal style established scat singing in jazz, and his personality was warm and engaging. Above all, he invested his music with great meaning. *Kansas City Jazz Museum, John Baker Collection.*

6

OVER his lifetime, Armstrong received almost two hundred awards in recognition for his outstanding musicality, including prestigious honors like the Grammy as well as honorary degrees and other commendations. Trumpet master Clark Terry paid this tribute to Louis: "I always think how amazing it is for a man like Pops to be as creative as he was. . . . He was to me like the pioneers in the old days who came through the territory. . . . He paved the way for all of us."

Kansas City Museum, Goin' To Kansas City Collection, Arthur McClure and Jennie Belle Peters.

butions to the world of jazz is overwhelming. His musical career spanned fifty years, during which time he pioneered innovative approaches to improvisation, developed virtuoso techniques for trumpet and cornet performance, defined new rhythmic and melodic devices, and gave jazz the soulful feeling known as swing.

Armstrong also exposed the world to the unique New Orleans vocal style known as scat singing.

Transcending racial stereotypes, attitudes, and prejudices, Armstrong reached out to all of America and to the world with his distinctive music and personality. Musicians often refer to him as "The First Messiah."

WITH his good looks, dapper style, and sophisticated personality, Duke Ellington always had an air of royalty. As a musician, his contributions as composer, arranger, band leader, and pianist are beyond category. His approaches to orchestration and composition were new and innovative, resulting in a sound that is uniquely "Ellington." Many consider him to be America's greatest twentieth-century musician. *Kansas City Jazz Museum, John Baker Collection.*

EDWARD KENNEDY "DUKE" ELLINGTON

Pianist, composer, arranger, orchestra leader
Born April 29, 1899, in Washington, D.C.
Died May 24, 1974, in New York City

Raised in turn-of-the-century Washington, Ellington had early private piano studies at home. Continuing to pursue music as a teenager, he found inspiration in the music of stride pianists Doc Perry and Louis Brown, who served as mentors. Henry Grant taught Ellington the principles of harmony, an experience which, he said, "lighted the direction to more highly developed composition." By 1918, Ellington had his own small group, The Serenaders.

In 1923, Ellington moved to the bustling community

T HE Duke Ellington Orchestra was internationally famous and introduced listeners around the world to the unique Ellington stylizations. One of Duke's famous sayings to the audience was "We do love you madly," and he could say it in over thirty languages! Over the five decades of its existence, the orchestra featured many outstanding musicians, including saxophonists Ben Webster (second from left, front row) and Harold Ashby, both from Kansas City. *Kansas City Jazz Museum, John Baker Collection.*

of Harlem in New York City, joining several friends in Elmer Snowden's Washingtonians. When Snowden left, Ellington took over and began his lifelong practice of tailoring arrangements to the individual styles of musicians. His band appeared at the Kentucky Club, where he composed for the various entertainment revues. The band's popularity led to an extended engagement at the Cotton Club, where the Duke Ellington Orchestra played from 1927 to 1931. Even though the club had a whites-only policy, Ellington's music reached listeners of all colors across the country through regular radio broadcasts. His unique new musical stylings led to increased popularity.

From there, Ellington gained national and then international visibility through recordings, broadcasts, film appearances, and European tours. He continued to expand and grow as a composer, creating popular songs such as "It Don't Mean a Thing if It Ain't Got That Swing" as well as larger works like *Symphony in Black*. His 1943 *Black Brown and Beige Suite* reflected on the various aspects of African American life in the United States. Over the next three decades, Ellington continued to lead a working orchestra, which traveled throughout the world performing his compositions and arrangements. Although most people would associate Ellington with big band swing orchestras, he wrote an astonishing array of music.

Inspired by African American music, as well as music from Europe, Asia, and Africa, he wrote symphonies, suites, comic operas, and tone poems, and he scored films, plays, and ballets. Late in life, he also composed and performed several celebrated sacred music concerts. He is credited with over two thousand compositions.

The Duke Ellington Orchestra was a sophisticated musical ensemble. It demonstrated that the music commonly known as jazz could be lyrical, complex, plush, and socially meaningful, as much of Ellington's music expressed the full range of African American life experiences. His innovative arrangements and orchestrations made major contributions to developing a broader concept of music as a medium of artistic expression.

According to his sister, Ruth, one of Duke's mottoes was "No boxes." His music transcended categories. He wore many musical hats: accomplished pianist, brilliant composer, and imaginative arranger.

Ellington did not like his music to be called jazz because he believed the term was too limiting. He often referred to his work as Negro folk music and drew from African American musical traditions such as spirituals, work songs, and blues to create new orchestral colors and sounds.

As an ever-evolving artist, astute businessman, and leading figure in African American culture, Ellington al-

E̲L̲L̲A̲ Fitzgerald was one of the most outstanding singers of the twentieth century. Her vocal musicianship featured bell-like clarity, flexibility of range, rhythmic brilliance, and clear enunciation of lyrics. She began her recording career with the Chick Webb Orchestra and gained national prominence with the hit 1938 recording, "A-Tisket, A-Tasket." *Duncan Scheidt.*

ways maintained an air of suaveness and sophistication, both in his music and his life. His public image was self-confident and assured, a major change from the stereotypical image of black musicians. His business savvy allowed him to sustain the orchestra for half a century, during which time it played an essential role in spreading his music worldwide.

Edward Kennedy "Duke" Ellington's music and personality were revered and celebrated in the over three hundred honors, recognitions, and awards bestowed upon him. Some of these include the NAACP Spingarn Medal for Achievement (1959), Ordem dos Musicos do Brasil Trophy (1968), the Presidential Medal of Freedom (1969), and the National Association of Negro Musicians Distinguished Service in Music Award (1972). He won eleven Grammys and numerous *Downbeat* and *Esquire* magazine polls. Ellington also received commendations and awards, including over seventeen honorary doctorates.

ELLA FITZGERALD

Singer and composer
Born April 4, 1917, in Newport News, Virginia
Died Saturday, June 15, 1996, in Beverly Hills, California

Ella Fitzgerald was born in Virginia, but her family soon relocated to Yonkers, New York. Orphaned at fifteen, she dreamed of becoming a dancer and singer. In 1934, at the age of seventeen, Ella tried her luck at an amateur-night contest in Harlem. When stage fright prevented her from dancing, she sang a piece popularized by singer Connee Boswell. The audience's enthusiasm encouraged her to continue singing. Her popularity grew, and she soon joined the Chick Webb Orchestra.

Ella Fitzgerald's work with drummer Chick Webb catapulted her into the national limelight. The orchestra's

ELLA'S distinctive and outstanding vocal scatting and phrasing were major contributions to bebop. She helped bridge popular music and jazz, expanding the audience for both forms. Through her numerous recordings and live performances, Ella influenced many singers and contributed to jazz consistently for more than sixty years. She is known as the First Lady of Song.

Kansas City Jazz Museum, John Baker Collection.

late 1930s hit recordings of "A-Tisket, A-Tasket," "Flat Foot Floogie," and "My Last Affair" featured her outstanding singing and led to her being recognized as one of the great vocalists of the swing era. When Webb died in 1939, she became the orchestra's leader, a rare opportunity for an African American woman.

As "modern jazz" expanded in the 1940s, so did Ella's musical brilliance. She responded to bebop with her own style of scat singing, which rivaled the work of the top jazz instrumentalists and earned her the respect of musicians and listeners alike. Over the next forty years, her work, including the legendary "songbook" recordings, clearly illustrated her incredible range of

vocal music skills. Her numerous recordings and live appearances thrilled audiences worldwide and provided first-hand witness as to why she was given the title of the First Lady of Song.

"Bell-like clarity, flexibility of range, clear enunciation of lyrics, rhythmic brilliance, vocal wizardry": These are just a few of the things that have been written about Ella Fitzgerald's singing. Her vocal achievements are outstanding. In bringing her unique virtuosity and creativity to jazz singing, Ella Fitzgerald influenced and inspired generations of younger singers. For over fifty years, she played a major role in bridging popular music and jazz, expanding the audience for both.

Shown here, third from the left, while a member of Billy Eckstine's band in the early 1940s, Charles Parker was a musician extraordinaire, combining a deep knowledge of Kansas City blues and jazz stylizations with virtuoso saxophone technique. Known as "Bird," Parker changed the way to play music forever with his exciting and pioneering improvisations. He was one of the creators of the approach to jazz improvisation now known as bebop. Lucky Thompson and Dizzy Gillespie are on the left, Eckstine on the right. *Larry Lester.*

CHARLES CHRISTOPHER "BIRD" PARKER

Saxophonist and composer
Born August 29, 1920, in Kansas City, Kansas
Died March 12, 1955, in New York City

Born in 1920, Charlie Parker grew up near Kansas City's thriving 18th and Vine district, where he was exposed to a distinctive brand of swinging blues. He developed his style during endless jam sessions, where he heard and learned from numerous musicians. His main mentor was alto saxophonist Henry "Buster" Smith, a master musician and veteran of such territory bands as the Oklahoma City Blue Devils. Parker earned the nickname "Yardbird" or "Bird" because of his fondness for eating chicken. In the early 1940s, as a member of Jay McShann's band, Parker's performances on recordings

became popular. When the band went to New York City in 1942, Parker decided to stay.

He joined in Harlem jam sessions featuring Dizzy Gillespie, Charlie Christian, Little Benny Harris, Coleman Hawkins, Thelonious Monk, Kenny Clarke, and Oscar Pettiford. These and other African American musicians were creating new approaches to jazz performance, setting the stage for "modern" jazz. Their music, often played at fast tempos, featured use of extended chord harmonies, complex melodies, and longer solos. When Parker joined them in 1942, he electrified listeners with breathtaking solos rooted in the Kansas City blues heritage.

After stints with the big bands of Earl Hines and Billy Eckstine, Parker and Gillespie formed a quintet that featured the new jazz performance styles labeled bebop. With his daring and exciting solos, supported by incredible saxophone virtuosity, Parker changed the way to

ALONG with being a great innovator, Parker also served as a mentor to younger musicians. Here he is seen with a young Miles Davis. In the late forties and early fifties, Parker often hired Davis to work in his band and provided many enriching music experiences that helped Davis develop into one of the great musicians.
Kansas City Museum, Goin' To Kansas City Collection, Duncan Scheidt.

play the music forever. In addition to working in small groups, Parker recorded with strings and Afro-Cuban groups. He also struggled with drug addiction during these years, leading to his untimely death in 1955.

Recognized as a genius, Charlie Parker was one of the most gifted and original performers in jazz. He transformed basic elements of African American blues through harmonic and melodic innovations and an incredible technique. His contributions to and achievements in jazz are unique and outstanding. Parker established a new approach to jazz performance, and his challenging compositions have become standards in the jazz repertoire.

Charlie Parker never received widespread popular or critical appreciation during his lifetime, but fellow musicians understood the brilliance of his innovative approach. Often, the artist is ahead of the general population, and this was true of Parker. Today, many years after his death, he is considered one of the greatest musicians of all time. He continues to influence musicians of all kinds, and recordings of his performances still sound immediate and fresh.

JAZZ MASTERS SELECTED DISCOGRAPHY

compiled by Eric Jackson

The following is a list of recommended recordings by the four jazz musicians profiled in this book.

LOUIS ARMSTRONG

1. *Louis Armstrong and King Oliver*
Milestone MCD-47017

2. *Louis Armstrong: Hot Fives*, vol. 1
Columbia CK-44049

3. *Louis Armstrong: Hot Fives*, vol. 2
Columbia CK-44253

4. *Louis Armstrong: Hot Fives*, vol. 3
Columbia CK-44422

5. *Louis Armstrong: Hot Fives*, vol. 4: *Louis Armstrong and Earl Hines*
Columbia CK-45142

6. *Louis Armstrong: Hot Fives*, vol. 5: *Louis in New York*
Columbia CK-46148

7. *Satchmo at Symphony Hall*
UNI/DECCA 11103-6612

8. *The Complete Louis Armstrong and Duke Ellington*
Blue Note B21y-93844

9. *Louis Armstrong: Stardust*
Portrait Masters RK-44093

10. *Louis Armstrong: Highlights from His Decca Years*
Decca GRD-2-638

DUKE ELLINGTON

1. *Duke Ellington: Concert of Sacred Music*
RCA (French) 74321192542

2. *Duke Ellington: The Blanton-Webster Band*
RCA 5659-2

3. *Early Ellington (1927–1934)*
Bluebird 6852

4. *Early Ellington: The Complete Brunswick and Vocalion Recordings*
Decca GRD 3-640

5. *Ellington at Newport*
Columbia CK-40587

6. *Ella at Duke's Place*
Verve 314529700

7. *Duke Ellington: 70th Birthday Concert*
Blue Note 746

8. *Duke Ellington: Far East Suite* (Special Mix)
Bluebird 66551-2

9. *Duke Ellington and John Coltrane*
Impulse IMPD 166

10. *Duke Ellington Uptown*
Columbia CK-40836

ELLA FITZGERALD

1. *Ella Fitzgerald: 75th Birthday Celebration*
Decca GRD 2-619

2. *Ella Fitzgerald: First Lady of Song*
Verve 314517898

3. *Ella Fitzgerald: The Early Years*, Part 1
Decca GRD-2-618

4. *Ella Fitzgerald: The Early Years*, Part 2
Decca GRD-2-623

5. *Ella in Rome: The Birthday Concert*
Verve 835454

6. *The Complete Ella in Berlin*
Verve 314-519564-2

7. *Ella Fitzgerald Sings the Cole Porter Songbook*
Verve 314537257-2

8. *Ella in London*
Pablo J33J 20033

9. *Ella Fitzgerald Sings the Duke Ellington Songbook*
Verve 837035

10. *Ella Fitzgerald*
Newport Jazz Festival
Columbia/Legacy 66809

CHARLIE PARKER

1. *Charlie Parker: The Complete Dial Sessions*
Jazz Classics JZCL 5010

2. *Charlie Parker with Strings: The Master Tapes*
Verve 314523984-2

3. *Charlie Parker Memorial*, vol. 1
Savoy Jazz SV-0101

4. *Charlie Parker Memorial*, vol. 2
Savoy Jazz SV-0103

5. *Immortal Charlie Parker*
Savoy Jazz SV-0102

6. *The Genius of Charlie Parker*
Savoy Jazz SV-0104

7. *Bird at the Roost, The Savoy Years—The Complete Royal Roost Performances*, vol. 1
Savoy Jazz SV-2259

8. *Charlie Parker: Jazz at Massey Hall*
Fantasy/OJC OJCCD-044

9. *Charlie Parker and Dizzy Gillespie—Bird & Diz*
Verve 314-521-436

10. *Charlie Parker: Swedish Schnapps*
Verve 849393-2

KANSAS CITY JAZZ

Three collections of different artists:

1. *The Real Kansas City*
Columbia/Legacy 64855

2. *Kansas City Legends*
Jazz Archives 5
EMP 158432

3. *Kansas City—Hot Jazz*
ABC Records 846222

4. Andy Kirk/Mary Lou Williams
Mary's Idea
Decca GRD 622

5. Bennie Moten
Basie Beginnings (1929–1932)
Bluebird 9768

6. Count Basie
The Complete Decca Recordings
Decca GRD 3-611

7. Jay McShann
Blues from Kansas City
Decca GRD 614

8. *The Essential Count Basie*, vol. 1
Columbia CK-40608

9. *Mary Lou Williams, 1927–1940*
Classics 630

Kansas City Jazz Museum, Clarence Love Collection.

16

JAZZ
AN INTERVIEW WITH JAY McSHANN

introduced and edited by Leonard Brown

R ECOGNIZED *as one of the great blues and jazz musicians of the twentieth century, Jay McShann (pianist, singer, composer, and band leader) has made major contributions to jazz and blues music for over sixty years. A Kansas City legend, he has appeared nationally and internationally during his career. The following interview with McShann, conducted in November of 1996 by Donna Lawrence Productions for use in the Kansas City Jazz Museum, provides insight into the life of one of the leading African American blues and jazz musicians in the Midwest. Reading about McShann's experiences presents many aspects of African American musical traditions, including how one learned the music; how musical performance styles were developed and transmitted; the problems of life on the road; what the jazz scene was like in and around Kansas City during the late 1930s and early 1940s, including local venues for performance; and how Kansas City jazz styles spread east, to New York. This interview has been edited for clarity and length.*

Born in Muskogee, Oklahoma, on January 12, 1909, McShann had an early exposure to music through the church. As he got older, he attended various performances held in school and occasional dances that featured many of the great territorial bands. One of his sisters studied piano, but he never took lessons. Even so, McShann "fooled around" at home with the piano and learned a few songs, but never took music seriously. Then, in his senior year of high school, McShann had an opportunity to play with the Gray Brothers, a small family band led by the father, who was also a band instructor.

EARLY YEARS (CIRCA 1927–1930)

I was living in Muskogee, Oklahoma. I had a chance to play with a small group called the Gray Brothers. It was a family band. They had a daughter that played drums and a daughter that played trombone. The boys played sax, trumpet, and drums. They would come get me to play jobs with them at different times. My folks were pretty strict on me and they were very particular about who they'd let me play with. Mr. Gray's being an old band instructor made it much better for me. I'd get a chance to make Christmas dates and New Year's dates and get a chance to see the other side, you know. I wanted to see what it was like bein' able to get out and play and not have two-minute restrictions. We were playing dances, mostly dances in these little towns. They had all kinda towns they played in, including Indian towns in Oklahoma.

After leaving their band I finished high school, and quite naturally after you finish high school you wanna get out. You wanna get out and try to see what's happenin'. So I wanted to leave Muskogee. I told my dad I was gonna leave. I wanted to see if I could make it on my own. He told me, "Well, if you get out there and you can't make it, you be sure and contact me and I'll get you back home."

I had an uncle in Tulsa, so I went to Tulsa. At that time the Gray Brothers Band was playing in a club called La Joann in Tulsa and they encouraged me to come to Tulsa. So I went. I'd been there a couple of weeks trying to get a job doing anything, but I couldn't get a job. Finally one day I heard a band rehearsing. I heard the sound of horns and followed the sound. When I stopped, it was upstairs. I didn't know whether to go up or not, you know, but I went on upstairs anyway. There were some doors and I walked in. The band was on the stand rehearsing, and people were sitting around. I just took a seat and listened.

Then I heard one of the guys say, "Well, we're gonna have to have a piano player for this weekend. We don't have a piano player." So I thought, Well I'll sit here and listen and see what they're doing, because I couldn't read music. So I sat and listened to them play four or five tunes down. After that, they were getting ready to break up rehearsal so I said, "Say, man, you all still need a piano player?" They said, "Yeah." I said, "I think I can make it." They said, "Well, man, why didn't you say something earlier?" I said, "Well, I just wanted to listen." They called some of those tunes they had played and that's what I was waiting for, to hear him call some of those tunes. Then they said, "Well, take off on something."[1] So I just took off on something; you know, just

something. They said, "Well, man, this cat can read and fake."[2]

PLAYING IN THE TERRITORIES (CIRCA 1930–1937)

Oh, they were nice places. Some places were called Winter Garden and things like that. I played dance halls all over Oklahoma. Guys like Bennie Moten had been playing halls for fifteen years. I didn't realize all of this, but those dance halls were there and were established. Territory bands covered all that territory because those halls were there with dances on Friday, Saturday, and Sunday nights. That's what we played, mostly dance halls.

Some of them were out in the country, especially when you got further north, like in the Dakotas, Nebraska, and Iowa. I played some places where it wasn't but three buildings there. The biggest building was the dance hall. We used to wonder, Who in the world is gonna come out here?

We'd be sitting around and it would start getting dark. We would start looking through the hills. You could see car lights when they would come over the hill.

Anyway, you go on in and get tuned up. It might be one or two people that would come and stand at the door looking in. Maybe somebody would be around the windows peepin' in. Then the band starts playing. In about fifteen minutes you have maybe fifteen couples in there. In about an hour you have about forty to fifty couples in there. As the night moves on, it loads up and the house is full. You wonder, Where did these people come from?

But people didn't think anything about going 150–200 miles to dance, back in those times. We used to talk to a lot of people. They'd say, "We came two hundred miles to see y'all."

GOING TO KANSAS CITY (1937)

I didn't realize that you came right through Kansas City going to Omaha. When we got to Kansas City, we had an hour and a half layover. I asked the cabbie at the bus station, "Man, how far is the Reno Club from

---

1. "Take off on something" means to spontaneously improvise.

2. "Read and fake" means having musical performance knowledge of written and oral traditions. The band was the Al Dennis Band. McShann joined and toured with it for the next few months.

here?" He said, "Just a couple of blocks, I'll show you and tell you exactly how to get there." So he told me and I said, "Well, you couldn't miss it." I said, "Is Basie still in town?" He says, "I think they are still in town." So I went down to this club and Basie had left, going east. Bus Moten had the band there.

When I walked in the club, some of the musicians recognized me. They hollered and called me. "Come on back to the bandstand, Mac." And I went on back to the stand.

So they said, "What are you doing in town?" I says, "Well, the club closed down in Kansas, and I decided to go up to Omaha to see my uncle." Bill Hadnott[3] said, "No, man, you don't wanna do that. . . . Look," he said, "Kansas City is the place. Stay right here in Kansas City." I said, "Well, man, I can't stay too long cause my bread's not that long." I said, "My bread[4] is short." Hadnott said, "Well, listen, I tell you what you do. Here, you take my keys and stay at my apartment, and I'll stay out to my girlfriend's house till you get a gig.[5] I'll guarantee you'll get a gig at the end of a day or two." I didn't believe him when he gave me that key, but I couldn't back down. So I took him at his word. I was staying at his apartment, and sure enough, in about a day or two, one of the old timers around here name Elmer Hopkins[6] was at the front door talking to the landlady. "Is there a musician around here called Mac Shane or McShane or something like that?" And when I heard him say that, I came out and said, "Yeah, here we are, right here." "Well, listen," he says, "are you working this weekend?" I said, "No, I'm not doing nothing." He says, "Well, I think I got a gig for you."

Hop's one of those guys who was always on top of the gigs, you know. There is usually one cat around town that knows where all the gigs are. They used the barbershop here in Kansas City as a meeting place or a calling place. Everybody called there for a band instead of calling the union.

Hop says, "Now, this gig, we only make a dollar and a quarter a night, but we through playing at one o'clock or one-fifteen." So we were through playing at one-fifteen and that would give me a chance to get around to all the other clubs and meet musicians, proprietors, and whatnot in different clubs and find out what was really happening in Kansas City.

THE KANSAS CITY SCENE

So that's how I got to Kansas City. And so, quite naturally, I stayed. I found out that they used to have a breakfast every morning at different clubs. These breakfasts started about five o'clock in the morning and would go on up to about eleven or twelve o'clock in the day. And I used to see a lot of guys that would be on their way to work with a dinner bucket. They would stop in a club and see all this going on and twelve o'clock would come and he would still be there at the club, just enjoying hisself. He doesn't realize how it happened, but it happened. He'd turn around and look to see what time it was and open his dinner bucket to eat his dinner, saying, "Well, I didn't make it today, I'll make it tomorrow." He missed his gig.

I worked with Hop for about a couple of weekends and then there was a big band. Henry "Buster" Smith had a big band at the Club Continental, which was at 12th and Wyandotte. Their piano player was in Denver and they had to have a piano player, so I went to work with them. I said I'd work with them until their piano player returned. So I worked with them until he returned and after he returned, instead of going back to the neighborhood club, I went to a club called Wolf's Buffet. There was just a piano and drums over there. That's all they had. He would bring in guys like Joe Turner to come in and sing the blues on the weekend.

But they never would hire no more than a piano and drums. Julia Lee was about the best moneymaker. She was the best piano player in town as far as making money, because she could play those money tunes. You know, there are certain tunes that we used to call money tunes around Kansas City. And if you didn't know those tunes, man, you were going to miss out on a lot of bread. Well, I found out right away that I had to learn a lot of these tunes I didn't like personally, myself. But I knew I would be lacking that bread, so I got busy and learned those tunes.

I found this out at the first breakfast dance I went to. It was a guy singing. He was an old favorite of Kansas City. The piano player and everybody had left the club, so he said, "Hey man, somebody says you play piano. You want to play for me and help me make some of this

---

3. Bill Hadnott was a Kansas City bass player.
4. "Bread" is an African American term for money.
5. "Gig" means a musical engagement or job.
6. Elmer Hopkins was a Kansas City drummer who gave McShann one of his first jobs in Kansas City.

money?" I say, "Yeah." So I got on the piano and he'd sing all over the club. We checked up after the breakfast dance was over. I think we made about $25 or $30 each.

So I says, "Man, any of them tunes that I tell you that I'm not familiar with, you go ahead and sing them and I'll catch up with ya the best I can." That was another way that I had of learning the tunes. I'd listen to what he was doing and then do as best I could to catch up. That worked out pretty good.

Well, when I got my own group, I went into the club on the Plaza. The Plaza was a good part of Kansas City and a moneymaking part of Kansas City. We got a chance to make bank at Martin's-on-the-Plaza.[7] I opened the Plaza and had about five people. I had a guy that we used to call "Gate." That's all I can remember was his nickname, Gate. Popeye on the alto, Gene Ramey on bass, and at that time I had Pete McShann on drums. I had already sent for Gus Johnson to come down from Ottumwa, Iowa. He had been up there working with Spec Red's group. Gus came in town and took Pete's place. After about the first week, Bird (Charlie Parker)[8] joined the group.

I had met Bird one night coming through town. He was at the Bar-Le-Duc, sitting in. As we passed by the club one night, we heard this guy blowing and we said, "Let's go in and see who this is blowing in here." So we went in and met him and we said, "Hey, man, where are you from?" He says, "I'm from Kansas City." I said, "Where have you been keeping yourself?" He says, "I been down in the Ozarks with George Lee's band. It's hard to get musicians to go down there and play because ain't nothing happening in the daytime. They say it's just a drag laying around in the day and nothing happening till at night when you get to the gig."

I said, "Well, where?" He said, "We was in the El." They was in Eldon, Missouri. He said he wanted to do some wood sheddin'.[9] So that's why he went down there with George Lee's band. I said, "Wood sheddin'? What do you mean, wood sheddin'?" He said, "Well, man, I wanted to get down there and try to catch up on my horn because I feel like I was lagging way behind musically and I wanted to try to catch up on my horn as best

I could. That's probably the reason you think I sound a little bit different." I said, "Yeah, you do sound different." That was our first meeting.

So after the first week I brought Bird in with the group and he stayed right there until the contract ran out.

BIRTH OF McSHANN'S BIG BAND

I knew if I put a big band together what I was gonna have to do. I was gonna have to have help. You got to have music to play. You got to have somewhere to play. You bring those guys in and they got to have somewhere to work. Everything depends on this, that, and the other. So these guys talked me into making that change, and I went for it. The same fella that got me the job in the Plaza is the same fella that bankrolled me to get this group together.

Anyway, I went on with this deal with Walter Bales backing me up.[10] I knew to go to Omaha and get musicians. They had a lot of good first men down there, and good first men are very valuable in a big band. I knew I was probably gonna have to go there to get the first men that I wanted, because there were more bands around there than here. The more musicians around, the better chance of getting the best first men.

In the meantime, things are going on around Kansas City. I got a chance to pick up on Joe Turner and Pete Johnson and that group of cats. Old Joe had worked with us up there at Wolf's. Joe would work with everybody, a different group every night in town. And Joe would come by and he'd tell Pete, "Roll 'em, Pete." Well, Pete played about fifteen minutes, he and the band. Then Joe would sing fifteen minutes. Then he'd tell 'em, "Roll 'em again, Pete." Pete rolled 'em again for another fifteen minutes. Joe would sing for another fifteen minutes with the band and then out, and that's the first number.

When you stop and look at it, the first number lasted one hour. I'm sitting up there waiting for these guys to run out of words and something to play. I've never seen nothing like that in Kansas and Oklahoma. These guys did one tune and it would last for an hour, and you would wonder where all the notes and words were coming from.

But Joe Turner had a way. He could just throw those words right off. As the music goes along he could do

---

7. McShann's band was the first African American and first jazz band to perform at Martin's-on-the-Plaza.

8. Bird was Charlie Parker's nickname.

9. Wood sheddin' means serious practicing on one's instrument.

10. Walter Bales was a local Kansas City businessman and jazz supporter.

it, you know. And he's always talked a lot of stuff, so it was no problem for him. Man, you started makin' a little trot to get in there.

So I got all the guys from out of town and brought them into Kansas City and took them to the club the first night we got there. I took them to the club where we were about to play and we just kind of let the guys play and jam around to see what different ones could do. We then figured out who would make the best first men.[11] We got all that figured out.

Now we got to go to work on this job. Now we're back at it again. No written music. We didn't have written music and so you got to start right back out again. So we started using our heads.[12] Then in the meantime, I got two arrangements and put them to work. We were playing for a walk-a-thon.[13] That's where you got a whole lot of people out on the floor walking and entertaining and you've got a judge out there who puts them through sprints. He would put them through all kind of obstacle courses, and the public would get enraged and say he's mean.

We'd have to keep twelve or fifteen policemen around there to keep them from beating the judge up. They had to keep two policemen with the judge so he could go to the rest room.

So by the time we finished that gig, we were ready to do a bunch of one-nighters. Well, starting out on the one-nighters, we didn't have any names, see. So, quite naturally, we played some gigs and nobody would be there. The promoter kept telling us, "Now wait a minute. Don't y'all give up so easy. Listen," he said. "Listen, the word is going to get around, and the next time you come you're going to have a big crowd." And you know, you got to go through a few of those things and pay a few dues. So we went through that part.

OUT OF KANSAS CITY AND ONE-NIGHTERS TO NEW YORK (1941)

We had recorded "Confessin' the Blues," and it just went like wildfire. Well, you know what that does. At al-most every place you played, you got to sell out. So that worked out beautiful for us because it pulled us out of that rut.

From then on we started doin' these one-nighters. So we had a guy on the stand named Clyde Bernhart. He's one of the old-timers. Clyde used to tell us, "Well, you guys play too many one-nighters. I'm gonna have to leave the band, and I'll join you when you get back to New York because I ain't never played this many one-nighters in my life." It was just straight one-nighters, you know. I think we did about sixty one-nighters straight. And he said, "It's just too much for me, so I'll see you back in New York."

We traveled all over the country, and finally we went east. We went to New York and played the Savoy Ballroom and did some theater dates. We did the Paradise in Detroit. We did the Washington circuit, Philadelphia, and Baltimore.

NEW YORK AND THE SAVOY BALLROOM

There used to be a bunch of dancers there in New York. They used to call them the Lindy Hoppers.[14] And what we were doing and what the Lindy Hoppers were doing just worked perfectly. It just went down so nice, you know? That's the reason we had such a long stay at the Savoy, because of the Lindy Hoppers. Redd Foxx was one of those Lindy Hoppers. The Lindy Hoppers really liked our music. We'd be playing up there at night, and the Lindy Hoppers would be doing all of this different stuff that they do right along with the music.

And they would get such an ovation from the people that was there. We were in there with Lucky Millinder's band one night. They went over to him and told him, "Lucky, I think you better come upstairs and see what's going on." So Lucky says, "Oh, I ain't worried about them Western dogs. I'll be up there; don't worry, don't let it bother you." Next set he went back downstairs to see Lucky again. He said, "Lucky, they told me to tell you, you better come up here and see what these Western dogs are doing."

So Lucky came out. I looked and saw Lucky over in the corner. We was playing about thirty minutes each

11. First men refers to instrumentalists who play the first or lead part in the orchestra or band.

12. Heads refers to musical arrangements conceived and created without written notation. In jazz, head arrangements were and are often composed spontaneously by members of the band.

13. Walk-a-thon refers to a type of marathon walking contest done to live music.

14. Lindy Hop was a popular dance of the time. Lindy Hoppers were the people who danced.

and we took about five or ten minutes of Lucky's band time. We had one of them type of tunes that we could do that, you know. So when we did that, then the house went crazy. It took about ten minutes for Lucky to get the house cooled down so that he could go on the stand. So by the time Lucky actually got on the stand and started playing, he only had a chance to play one or two numbers. When he finished those one or two numbers, we was raring you know; we was waiting for him. It got Lucky kind of bumfuzzled.[15] It really kind of turned him around because Lucky was playing the wrong stuff.

See, we were swinging and that's what the Hoppers was doing. They were swinging and we were swinging. Lucky wanted to go another way, but it was the wrong way, see. The crowd went for what was happening with the Lindy Hoppers and the band, you know. That's what they wanted. And we was lucky enough to be the ones there playing it, so we get a little bit of the credit. After that they changed us from number-two bandstand to number one. And we stayed number one the whole time we was there. Yeah.

THE UNIQUENESS OF THE KANSAS CITY SOUND

Well, I'll tell you this. It seems to me that when they speak about the Kansas City sound, I think they more or less are talking about the instruments. When those instruments are playing, they are singing. When we used to rehearse, we'd tell them, "Sing them notes." You know, just like you're singing it. Well, when that reed section and that brass section get to singing alike, you got a great sound going. And that's where the great sound comes from, from singing it.

You see, Kansas City always did have a feeling for music. Even their singers always had a great feel. And it's surprising how a lot of people might not realize it.

When I was little, my dad used to take me to what they called singing conventions. That's where all the churches of the different towns would meet up. They'd have a church from over here, a church from over there, a church from that town, maybe fifteen or twenty singing groups. Dad would take me to those singing conventions, and boy, I heard more good singing and I liked it.

I used to sit on the bench with some of them old guys,

15. Bumfuzzled means confused.

and there'd be a great bass singer and he'd be singing bass so low I could feel the bench shake. That's a fact. And I noticed all that when I was coming up as a kid.

Then I used to listen to how they would phrase. You get used to listening to a certain sound. Listening to those sounds, I always enjoyed it. I think that helped me learn to appreciate certain things.

You see, it's just like swinging real hard and then they go to a church mood. And you recognize those right off, soon as they hit those different moods and things. When it's—you know—done right and the mood's there, it's quite captivating. I can understand why it makes some people holler. When it hits right, it's right.

ON CHARLIE "BIRD" PARKER

Charlie was with me from 1939 to '40, '41, '42, '43, and part of '44; that's about four years.

All the time Bird was with us, he was hearing these other sounds. He liked playing with the group but that didn't keep him from hearing those sounds. He's going to hear what he's going to hear. So gradually, after he left the band, he went on to the sound that he had been hearing. He was able to hear a lot of sounds that so many of the musicians couldn't hear back then.

Yeah, it was a matter of hearing it, and he heard it, and he wasn't the only one that heard it. There have been a lot of guys that have come along since him that heard something. It wasn't all the same, but they were all hearing it.

Everybody doesn't have the same thing and everybody can't deal with the same thing the same way. It's going to come from another direction. The thing that he's hearing comes from a completely different direction with somebody else.

KANSAS CITY JAZZ AS A REFLECTION OF LIFE

Well, I think what was coming out had to be a reflection of the time. When people listened to the blues, they were listening to Joe Turner. They listened because they wanted to hear every word he said. He might go into a thing, "That's all right, baby, that's all right for you. That's all right, baby, that's all right for you. That's all right, baby, just any old way you do. Don't the moon look pretty shining down through the trees." Well, they want to hear what's going to follow that, so they carried the tune along with it. They know the tune he's doing, but they want to hear what he's going to say with the tune. "Don't my baby look good coming home with me? Eyes like diamonds, teeth like Klondike gold."

The blues tells the truth because it's the thing that the blues is about. You got all kind of blues, but they're still the blues. Joe Turner was one of the main blues singers out of Kansas City that put it down. That's the way he did it, and I think it's just like a religion, in a way to speak.

There was a lot of people that said, "Now don't come in here playing none of that bop[16] stuff." They'd tell the band, "Don't come in here with none of this bop stuff. We don't want to hear it."

We would play it because it was already there. We already had it in the music. It would be in the ordinary songs we were playing. It was there so people could listen to it. The next thing they knew, people were liking bop because it did certain things that they liked.

Sometimes people take a long time before they get the feel of what's happening. I always loved Louis Armstrong's blowing. Louis Armstrong, the trumpet player—Satchmo. I loved his playing, but when I was a kid I didn't like his singing. After I got grown, I was listening one night and he was singing a number. And boy,

that turned me on. I said to someone, "Who is that singing?" They said, "That's Louis Armstrong." I said, "No, it can't be." They said, "Yes, it is." I looked at the record and it was Armstrong. I thought it was the greatest thing I had ever heard him do: "Blueberry Hill."

It took me all those years, and I heard him do all kinds of songs.

ON YOUTH, MUSIC, AND LIFE

It's just like kids, now. They've got to give those kids a break. They talk about them liking rock 'n' roll, this and that and the other. You've got to give the kids a break because they have to grow up. A kid's got to like the things that kids are going to like when he's coming up. He's got to go through that experience, whatever it is. They say it's loud, rock 'n' roll. He's got to hear it loud. He wants to rock 'n' roll and that's it. Let him have it. Don't stop him. The mistake is in stopping him. Don't stop him, let him go.

This goes along with life. A lot of times we don't like to accept it as life, but that means that music is life. It tells the stories of life and it goes along with life.

That's the reason a lot of people say, "Well, I don't know what we'd do without music. What would we be doing?" We'd be going crazy, I guess. I don't know. But that's a fact, see. You know they say it settles the beast. If it settles the old beast down, it should help us. Yeah.

---

16. Bop refers to advanced styles of jazz performance that were created in the late 1930s and early 1940s.

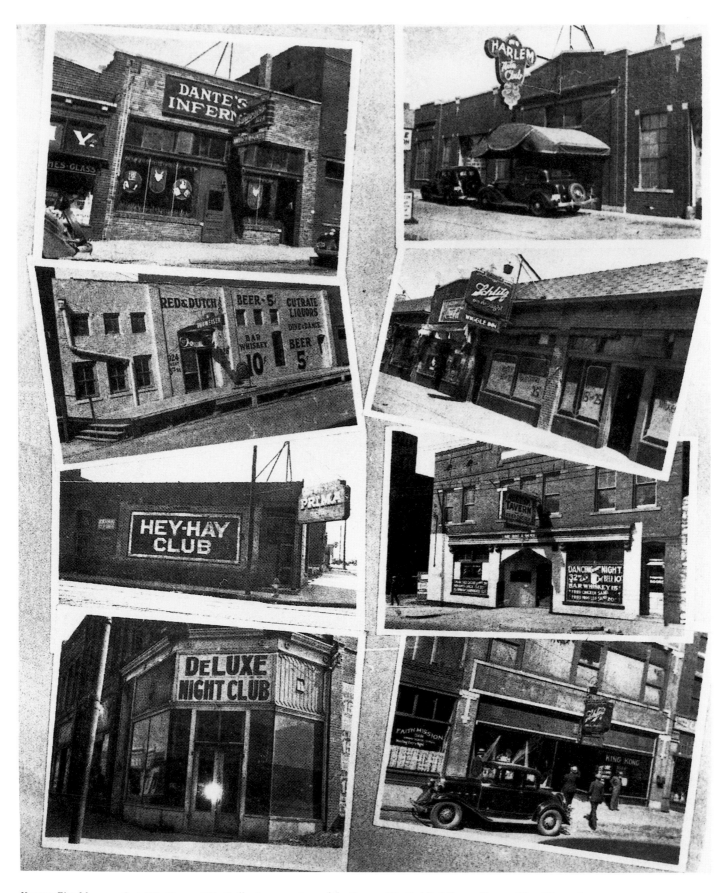

Kansas City Museum Goin' To Kansas City Collection, courtesy of the Kansas City Public Library, Kansas City, Missouri.

24

JAZZ

KANSAS CITY NIGHTCLUBS AND CLUB LIFE

by Claude Page

FROM THE perspective of today's Kansas City, it is difficult to imagine the swinging town of the 1930s when jazz musicians numbering in the hundreds played clubs and dances all over town. Kansas Citians had their pick of jazz, blues, and ragtime, sweet or hot, in tiny joints or in large glittering dance halls. In the middle of the Great Depression, Kansas City was jumping with jazz. Local folks went out nightly (sometimes all night) to dance and party. They started in the 1920s and partied right through the Depression and into the 1940s.

Much has been written about Kansas City as a wide-open town during the Pendergast years. From 1925 to 1938, Tom Pendergast's political machine ran the city efficiently, but with crime—particularly liquor, gambling, and vice—as a profitable sideline. Lax enforcement of liquor laws encouraged clubs to stay open. As the clubs proliferated, Kansas City became a mecca for jazz musicians, who arrived from all over the Midwest.

There were other reasons for the rise of KC nightlife. One was the swelling of the city's African American population after the turn of the century, and especially during World War I. In the great migration from the South, Kansas City was a stopping-off point, and many stayed. Between 1900 and 1940, Kansas City's African American population more than doubled, from 17,567 to 41,574.

Kansas City's central geographic location for bands and musical troupes crossing the country didn't hurt, either. The city was the westernmost stop for the TOBA (Theater Owners' Booking Association) group of theaters featuring African American acts. Traveling companies, in fact, were often stranded in town (which is how Count Basie, from Red Bank, New Jersey, became a Kansas Citian).

Social clubs played a large part in the lives of African Americans and in the growing popularity of jazz. The clubs provided a social outlet that was otherwise unavailable in a segregated community. The rise of dance halls and jazz bands paralleled the growth of social clubs. By 1937, everyone had joined; notices from over eighty separate clubs appeared weekly in the *Kansas City Call*, and each club gave its share of dances.

"Everybody belonged to a club. Why, we went to dances two or three nights a week," Irene Marcus remembers. "Sometimes all night. The Co-eds would have a dance at nine o'clock, the Beau Brummels a Midnight Ramble, and then the Sans Soucis would have a breakfast dance. When did we sleep? We didn't. We were young and having too much fun. The clubs and church were our social life, and we were out every night. The kids today don't have the society we did."

In Kansas City, the nightclubs and dance halls were spread all over town. Downtown, the swanky College Inn was at 12th and Baltimore, with the Mint and the Beetle Taxi Dance Hall close by. Barney Google's was at 9th and Grand, but the biggest splash of clubs was on 12th and Cherry. Here were the 600 Club, the Ace, the Reno, King Kong Lair, the Nut House, Amos 'N' Andy's, Greenleaf Gardens, and Dante's Inferno. Close by at

ENO Club, c.1937. Bill Searcy is at the piano, Christyanna Buckner is the vocalist, and Curtyse Foster is at sax, to the left of the kitty. The Reno advertised an "All-colored continuous floor show." The players didn't earn much, however. Oliver Todd, who closed the club in 1938, made $3 a night. His band members made $2.50, plus $4 to $5 apiece from the kitty. *Kansas City Jazz Museum, Tanya Foster Collection.*

12th and Troost were Martini's and the Spinning Wheel.

Milton Morris's Hey-Hay Club, decorated with cornstalks on walls and ceiling (patrons sat on bales of hay) was at 4th and Cherry, the Bar-Le-Duc was at 5th and Main, and the Nite After Nite at 8th and Charlotte. South of downtown, spots included the Stork Club at 17th and Baltimore; the Dump at 26th and McGee; the Wiggle Inn at 26th and Troost; the Trocadero, Movie Chateau, and Casa Fiesta at 39th and Main; and Martin's-on-the-Plaza, where Jay McShann played an extended engagement. Tootie's Mayfair was way out south, at 7836 Wornall.

The nightclubs just listed were small white clubs where jazz bands frequently played. Large dance halls included the Pla-Mor Ballroom at 30th and Main, the El Torreon Ballroom at 31st and Gillham, and Fairyland Park at 75th and Prospect.

A group of clubs in Hicks Hollow, on Independence close to Charlotte, were often rough-and-tumble affairs and are spoken of fondly. These were the Hawaiian Gardens, the Black and Tan, the Hole in the Wall, the Backbiter's Club, the first Dante's Inferno, and the Honolulu Moon.

Even more numerous than the white clubs, African American clubs of the thirties and forties were located generally east of Paseo on 12th and 18th streets. The Lone Star, Sunset, Havana Inn, Boulevard Room, and Orchid Room were the main niteries close to 12th and Vine. The main 18th Street clubs were the Yellow Front, Paseo Tap Room, Blue Room, the Subway, Fox's, Wolf's

WOODIE Walder's Kentucky Club Swing Unit, c.1937. Johnny Thomas's Kentucky Barbecue, at 19th and Vine, was a magnet for younger players, as well as Walder's accomplished aggregation. From left: Elbert "Coots" Dye, Woodie Walder, Jack "Snake" Johnson, Herman Walder, Bill Martin, Bill Terry, Baby Lovett. This restaurant, later purchased by George Gates, would be the first Gates barbecue. *The Kansas City Call.*

Buffet, the Elk's Rest, El Capitan, Scott's Theater Restaurant, Lucille's Paradise, and the Zelmaroda. Nearby were the Cherry Blossom, at 1822 Vine, and the Kentucky Barbecue and Mardi Gras, at 19th and Vine.

Dance halls included the Labor Temple at 14th and Woodland; Lyric Hall, 1731 Lydia (above Watkins Family Undertakers); Paseo Hall, 15th and Paseo; Lincoln Hall, at 18th and Vine; and Dreamland Hall, 22nd and Vine. Two spots outside of town on 40 Highway were Penrod, to the west, and the Nu 40 Inn, due east.

The nightclubs were often as colorful as the personali-

ties who operated them. Piney Brown ran the Sunset Crystal Palace, a modest club on 12th Street at Highland. Brown was a benevolent gentleman, who lent a helping hand to musicians and was also allied with gambling and vice interests. "He was a pimp, you know," says singer Myra Taylor.

The Sunset was home to Joe Turner and Pete Johnson, the singer and the piano player who would take the KC sound to New York in 1938. Turner would shout the blues in the Sunset and then continue singing out into 12th Street, "calling the children home," as Turner said. "Joe would sing right out the door, and

CELESTER White's band at the Zelmaroda Club. From left: Eddie Saunders, saxophone; Jack Jackson, bass; Paul Oliver; trumpet; White, drums; Sonny Kenner, guitar. Emmitt Scott opened the Zelmaroda at 18th and Euclid just after the Second World War; by 1948, when this picture was taken, the genial Mose Covington was the owner. *The Kansas City Call.*

JOE Thomas at the Beau Brummel Club, c.1954. Thomas, the famous Jimmie Lunceford tenor, moved to Kansas City in the early fifties, leading small combos. The Beau Brummels, a social club in existence for over fifty years, renovated the former Lyric Hall at 1731 Lydia for their clubhouse. Since the 1920s, the hall had been the scene of countless dances; for years, it was the regular spot to hear George E. Lee. Little did the dancers care that the hall was on the second floor, above Watkins Family Undertakers! *Kansas City Jazz Museum, Oliver Todd Collection.*

T HE Blue Room, St. Joseph, c.1940. This club is remembered as a swinging 4th Street spot in St. Joseph, along with the equally popular Frog Hop Ballroom. Clifford Love is at the drums leading this group. Love played with the Count Basie, B. C. Kynard, and Charles Green bands. *The Kansas City Call.*

even the people on the streetcar going by would be hopping," recalls Oliver Todd.

When he wasn't playing the Sunset, Turner was generally across the street at the Lone Star, a club run by Frank Duncan, the famous Kansas City Monarchs catcher. At one time married to Julia Lee, Duncan and the Monarchs were celebrities on the local jazz scene.

Claude Williams had the band that opened Lucille's Paradise in 1936, but the personality who drew the patrons was Lucille Webb, who hosted the nightclub on 18th Street at Highland. Always in chic attire, Lucille continually improved the establishment, expanding and even originating a local radio broadcast. " She was quite an elegant lady, and a very nice person," recalls 18th Street barber Clarence Ware.

The Cherry Blossom, at 1822 Vine, had a short life in the early thirties but was home to Count Basie and his Cherry Blossom Orchestra, Basie's first group, which featured Jimmy Rushing as a strolling blues singer. The club, decorated as a Japanese garden complete with palm trees, was the former Eblon Theater, where Basie had played piano for silent pictures in the 1920s. As the Cherry Blossom, and later as the Chez Paree, the club was the scene of many jam sessions into the 1940s. In the 1950s, it was renovated and reopened as the Monarch Bowl.

Lucille's, the Cherry Blossom, and the Subway were after-hours favorites for musicians to meet for jam sessions. The Subway was a tiny club in the basement of 1416 East 18th Street, where past a doorman and down

BENNIE Brooks and Mary, El Capitan. The El Cap, named after the railroad line, opened in 1946 at 1614 East 18th Street. Besides the lively atmosphere, one of the club's main attractions was Merl Reed, the singing bartender. Brooks was a popular sporting gentleman on 18th Street. *Kansas City Jazz Museum.*

THESE wartime dancers were enjoying Celester White's Orchestra, at Mose Covington's Zelmaroda Club, at 18th and Euclid.
Kansas City Jazz Museum, Marcellus Hughes Collection.

THE inscription on the back of this picture reads, *Frank's Place. Christmas Eve, 1934.* Although most of the 12th Street clubs were truly joints, the tablecloths and patrons' smart attire in this venue are exceptional.
Kansas City Jazz Museum, Claude Page Collection.

CLARENCE Love and his orchestra, The Jail, c.1932. Mary Lou Williams remembers playing after hours with Jack Teagarden in this downtown speak: "It was decorated to resemble the inside of a penitentiary, with bars on the windows and waiters in striped uniforms like down-South convicts." *Kansas City Jazz Museum, Clarence Love Collection.*

DANCERS at the Chez Paree, c.1939. Christyanna Buckner is at the center of this line; the Chez Paree's floor show was choreographed by Hollywood-trained Joe Stevenson. Stevenson's wife Ethelynn is at far left, and Vashti Collins is second from right. Other dancers were picked, literally off the street, and trained by Stevenson for the chorus. *The Kansas City Call.*

Dancer Marsha Bland began her career in the 1940s at Scott's Theater Restaurant, which was then located at the southeast corner of 18th and Highland. Emmitt Scott advertised "Entertainment Up-to-Date for the Sedate." Scott's featured a full floor show, and Bland remembers being "just a kid, but the show was fantastic." *Kansas City Jazz Museum, Marsha Bland Collection.*

Eddie Saunders and Lucky Enois at the Orchid Room on 12th Street, 1954. Richard "Corky" Jackson is on drums, with Jack Lewis on bass. *The Kansas City Call.*

a narrow stairway were the swingingest jam sessions in town. "I remember once at the Subway Club," recalled pianist Sammy Price, "I came by a session at about ten o'clock and then went home to clean up and change my clothes. I came back a little after one o'clock and they were still playing the same song."

On 18th Street, Emmitt Scott operated classy nightclubs, with full floor shows and often dinner and dancing. Scott's Theater Restaurant was the finest of many establishments that came and went in the old Boone Theater at 18th and Highland. Scott later started the Zelmaroda Club, at 18th and Euclid.

Often a bartender's personality would make a club's reputation—and create a loyal following. Jesse

"Kingfish" Fisher was a famous mixologist on 12th Street and later at Street's Blue Room, an elegant establishment in Reuben Street's Hotel on 18th Street. John "Johnny Cake" Walker made a reputation at the Boulevard Room, at 12th and Paseo.

The Reno Club, at 12th and Cherry, is the most storied in KC jazz history. Small in size, the Reno was a whites-only club. "It was run by gangsters, you know. But there was no trouble," recalls Myra Taylor. Prostitutes plied their trade in the club, using rooms upstairs, and musicians smoked joints out back, where legend says marijuana grew wild.

Sol Stibel, the Reno's manager, booked Count Basie in 1935. Basie and his Barons of Rhythm were a huge hit,

*O*N a return visit to Kansas City, Count Basie jams with Claiborne "Frog" Graves, saxophone; Baby Lovett, drums; and Jimmy Hill, guitar, c.1940. Decoration in many clubs was minimal, as this photo attests. *Kansas City Jazz Museum, Mattie Story Collection.*

and radio station W9XBY broadcast the group live from the Reno; jazz writer John Hammond heard Basie on his car radio from Chicago. Seeing the band in person at the Reno, Hammond said, "was the most exciting musical experience I can remember."

There was no cover charge at the Reno, says Oliver Todd, whose band was the last to play the club in 1938. Todd made under $10 a night playing the Reno, at shows that "started at ten o'clock and midnight. We played till the crowd went home"—which might be one o'clock or late the next day.

In the 1920s and 1930s, music was frequently scheduled around the clock. When Walter Knight's band played the Sunset Club in 1938, shows started at eleven o'clock Friday and ran until three-thirty Saturday afternoon. Saturday midnight shows, called Break O'Day dances, were a popular Bennie Moten feature at Paseo

Hall in the late twenties. Breakfast dances began at eight on a weekday morning, and a special Sunday-night ramble began at midnight Sunday, starting the week off right.

Liquor, of course, was a feature of Kansas City's nightclubs, even during Prohibition. But the accompaniment to jazz most remembered was the hot shrimp and crawfish boiled at the clubs on 12th and 18th streets in the 1930s. Writer Dave Dexter Jr. recalled "the tall Armour & Co. lard can . . . filled with shrimps or freshwater crayfish. . . . Did Escoffier ever prepare so tantalizing a dish?" Hot corn and potatoes often accompanied the crawdads. Right outside the clubs, vendors sold their wares to passersby. Chili parlors also lined 12th and 18th streets; Dexter refers to Charlie Parker as an avid chili gourmet until he died. And, of course, barbecue: "Only the finest in the whole hog-lovin' world," as Mary Lou Williams is quoted as saying.

J<small>AM</small> session at the Flamingo Club, in Kansas City, Kansas, c.1942. Granville Harris is in front on sax at this informal session; Oliver Todd, trumpet, and Bill Jones, are at left, and Gene Carter is on saxophone at right. Pianist Nessie Johnson is at the microphone at center. *Kansas City Jazz Museum, Oliver Todd Collection.*

JAMMING at the Chez Paree, early 1940s. In front are trumpets Oliver Todd and Gerald Hunter; saxophones are Jimmie Keith, Raymond Ice, Granville Harris, and Cleophus Berry; at right is bassist Roy Johnson. This is clearly a late-night session, with the players dressed from their earlier gigs. *Kansas City Jazz Museum, Oliver Todd Collection.*

RENO Club, 1940. The exterior of the famous club, "The House of Swing." The Reno opened with the repeal of Prohibition in 1933. By 1938, with the police clampdown on 12th Street clubs, the Reno was gone.
Kansas City Landmarks Commission.

ERNEST Daniels band, c.1942. This bandstand is typical of many in the joints of the era. Daniels is at the drums, with Franz Bruce under the clock and John Church to his left.
The Kansas City Call.

KANSAS CITY JAZZ:
A PHOTOGRAPHIC HISTORY

captions by Claude Page

ASSEMBLED bands at the Musicians' Union, 1930. The occasion was the annual Battle of the Bands at Paseo Hall and a parade to wind up at the new union building, 1823 Highland. The union boasted 347 members (it started in 1917 with 25), and most of them were part of the parade. The eight contestants were Bennie Moten and George Lee's orchestras, Elmer Payne's Music Masters, Paul Banks's Rhythm Aces, Andy Kirk's 12 Clouds of Joy, Jap Allen's Troubadours, Julius Banks's Red Devils, and Bill Little and His Little Bills (a Moten unit). *Kansas City Jazz Museum, Leroy "Buster" Berry Collection.*

T HE thirteen Original Blue Devils. Although not the "original" version of this seminal band (Bennie Moten had lured away many of the Devils by this time), these 1932 Devils featured Lester Young, Buster Smith, and Ernie Williams as leader. From left: Leroy "Snake" White, George Hudson, Theodore Ross, Leonard Chadwick, Lester Young, George Young, Ernie Williams, Buster Smith, Charles Washington, Reuben Lynch, Druie Bess, Abe Bolar, Ray Howell. "The greatest band I ever heard in my life," said Basie drummer Jo Jones, "was Walter Page's Blue Devils." *Kansas City Museum, Goin' To Kansas City Collection, Duncan Scheidt.*

THE Bennie Moten Orchestra at Fairyland Park, c.1931. The band was at its most popular and had just recorded its best sides, with Count Basie, Hot Lips Page, Ed Lewis, Eddie Durham, Woodie Walder, Leroy Berry, Harlan Leonard, and Jack Washington (bottom: second, third, fourth, sixth, seventh, eighth, ninth, and twelfth from left). At top are Bennie Moten, Bus Moten, and James Rushing. *Kansas City Jazz Museum, Leroy "Buster" Berry Collection.*

THE fourteen-piece Moten aggregation relaxing in Kansas City, c.1932. Jimmy Rushing is at left, Basie is fourth from left, and Bennie Moten is at right. *Duncan Scheidt* (Opposite page)

*C*OUNT Basie and soloists, Apollo Theater, New York, 1937. From left: Eddie Durham, guitar; Herschel Evans, tenor sax; Basie, piano; Benny Morton, trombone; Lester Young, tenor sax; Buck Clayton, trumpet; Walter Page, bass. Billie Holiday was singing with the band at this time, although she didn't record with the group. *Frank Driggs.*

H AZEL Scott with Count Basie and the orchestra, c.1942. Helen Humes, Basie's longtime vocalist, had just left the band, and Scott was sitting in at this New York date. *Archive/Metronome.*

THUGS BALL

given by the Samper Fidelis Girls

REGAL GRILL. 2451 BROOKLYN

Friday, April 1, 1938   Hrs 9 until ?

ADMISSION   — 15c

ORAN "Hot Lips" Page is an unsung creator of the Kansas City sound of the 1930s. Originally from Dallas, Page joined half brother Walter Page's Blue Devils in 1928 and came to Kansas City to play with Moten and then Basie at the Reno Club. Basie, in his understated way, said Page "took care of a lot of jazz on trumpet." In the riff-based head arrangements of Moten and Basie, Page soloed and laid down the riff, chorus after chorus, for the band to follow. In large measure, the driving sound of the Basie band was due to Page. He left Basie in 1936 and went east to be a leader of his own groups. *The Kansas City Call.*

JUNE Richmond with a later Andy Kirk orchestra, c.1942. Richmond replaced Pha Terrell as vocalist with Kirk; also in the band at this time were trumpets Harold "Shorty" Baker and Howard McGhee. Baker gained most renown later with Duke Ellington, and McGhee, after recording "McGhee Special" with Kirk, went on to be a major bop influence. *The Kansas City Call.*

Lammar Wright, a Lincoln High graduate, was with Bennie Moten's original six-piece band in 1921, later soloing on "South," Moten's 1924 hit. He played first trumpet with Cab Calloway and was featured with Don Redman, Lucky Millinder, Louis Armstrong, and others. *Kansas City Jazz Museum, VeEssa Spivey Collection.*

Bus Moten, Leroy "Buster" Berry, and Jimmy Rushing, c.1933, Kansas City. Berry's guitar and banjo work are solid features of the Moten band's 1929–32 recordings. Rushing, first with the Blue Devils and then with Moten and Basie, typified a relaxed and swinging sound that was unmistakably Kansas City. He sang with Basie until 1950. *Kansas City Jazz Museum, Leroy "Buster" Berry Collection.*

WILLIAM "COUNT" Basie in his first professional band, Harry Richardson's Sunny Kings of Syncopation, Red Bank, New Jersey, 1922. From left: Jimmy Hill, Basie, Elmer Williams, Harry Richardson. *Frank Driggs.*

COUNT Basie swinging the orchestra, 1942, Strand Theater, New York. This is the powerhouse band that carried the Kansas City sound nationwide: Buck Clayton, Ed Lewis, Al Killian, Harry Edison, trumpets; Vic Dickenson, Dan Minor, Dicky Wells, trombones; Lester Young, Earl Warren, Buddy Tate, Jack Washington, saxophones; and the surging rhythm section of Basie: Freddie Green, guitar; Jo Jones, drums; and Walter Page, bass. Jimmy Rushing was the featured vocalist. *Frank Driggs.*

LESTER Young, a major innovator and influence on the tenor saxophone, began his Kansas City career in 1930 with the Blue Devils. He played briefly with Clarence Love, Bennie Moten, and Andy Kirk and then joined Count Basie at the Reno Club in 1936. Young was with Basie until 1940, making what many consider his greatest recordings; along with Coleman Hawkins, Young was the most innovative tenor in jazz. Billie Holiday named him Prez: the president of the tenor saxophone. *The Kansas City Call.*

E DDIE Durham, though a trombonist and guitar player of note, made his greatest mark as an arranger and composer. He played with Paul Banks, the Blue Devils, and Bennie Moten; when he began arranging for Moten, "Moten Stomp" became "Moten Swing." The band started jumping, and Durham later arranged for Count Basie, Jimmie Lunceford, and Glenn Miller. In the 1940s, he was musical director of the International Sweethearts of Rhythm and other bands. *The Kansas City Call.*

E ARL Warren and Samuel "Baby" Lovett, Basie band. Lovett filled in for an ill Jo Jones in the Basie band; he poses here, on the road in New York, with ace alto sax player Earl Warren, who was with Basie from 1937 to 1945.
The Kansas City Call.

Kansas City Jazz Museum, John Baker Collection.

George E. Lee's Singing Novelty Orchestra, 1922. Lee, on baritone sax, sang with his band, as did his sister, Julia. Lee began in 1920 and ruled Kansas City clubs with Moten until 1933. Popular because of its showmanship, this band was a dancers' favorite. Note the musical saw leaning on Julia's piano. *Kansas City Museum, Goin' To Kansas City Collection, Charles Goodwin.*

AFTER leaving George Lee's band, Julia Lee struck out on her own with small groups, achieving greater renown than her brother. Her swinging piano and vocal style were favorites in Kansas City clubs for over twenty years. *Kansas City Jazz Museum, John Baker Collection.*

LEE was the feature at a 1949 recording session in Los Angeles with (from left) Baby Lovett, Vic Dickenson, Benny Carter, Dave Cavanaugh, Jack Marshall, and Bill Hadnott. Dave Dexter Jr. set up all-star sessions with Lee; they paid off with some fine sides for Capitol Records. This was the year Lee and Baby Lovett played the Truman White House.
Kansas City Jazz Museum, Mattie Story Collection.

ANDY Kirk's band in the newly rebuilt Fairyland Park pavilion, c.1933. Prominent soloists were saxophonist Dick Wilson (top right), trumpeter Irving "Mouse" Randolph (fourth from left), and, of course, the trucking Mary Lou Williams.
Kansas City Museum, Goin' To Kansas City Collection.

WHEN Andy Kirk's pianist, Marion Jackson, couldn't make a 1929 Brunswick Records audition, saxophonist John Williams's wife, Mary Lou, sat in, and history was made. "The Lady That Swings the Band" headlined Kirk's orchestra and then gained fame as a composer, arranger, and performer. *The Kansas City Call.*

To VeEssa your loveliness is hard To surpass— Sincere [signature] 6/7/...

PHA Terrell's vocalization of "Until the Real Thing Comes Along," a solid hit in 1936, took Kirk's band to the Grand Terrace Ballroom in Chicago, where a nationwide radio audience sent it to greater heights. This would be Kirk's theme song until the band's demise in 1946. *Kansas City Jazz Museum, VeEssa Spivey Collection.*

By the time Charlie Parker, center, traveled to Wichita, Kansas (at radio station KFBI in this photo), to make his first recordings with Jay McShann, he was actually a seasoned Kansas City veteran. This was November of 1940, and Parker had previously worked with Laurence Keyes, Jimmie Keith, Tommy Douglas, and Harlan Leonard. Parker and McShann are at the brink; after this point, the orchestra, with its star soloist, took off. *Jay and MaryAnn McShann.*

JAY McShann relaxing with a later band, c.1955. McShann is at lower left, with David "Daahoud" Williams whispering in his ear, Larry Cummings (now Luqman Hamza), Betty Bryant, Ahmaad Aladeen, and Al Duncan at Mose Covington's Top Hat Grill on 18th Street. *Jay and MaryAnn McShann.*

Kansas City Jazz Museum, John Baker Collection.

A LONG with being one of the greatest musicians of all time, Parker was a regular guy in Kansas City, with a reputation for expressing humor with his fellow musicians. *Frank Driggs.*

A swinging McShann band at the Savoy Ballroom, New York, January 1942. The success of "Confessin' the Blues," with Walter Brown's laconic vocal, got the band national engagements; Brown's vocalizing on the song got wide publicity, at the expense of the more swinging instrumentals in the band's book. *Goin' To Kansas City Collection, courtesy of the Kansas City Museum, Kansas City, Missouri, and Gene Ramey.*

Kansas City Jazz Museum.

*C*LARENCE Love Orchestra, c.1931. Love's band, with a swinging sweet sound reminiscent of Andy Kirk's, held its own in Kansas City and the territories. Lester Young, Tommy Douglas, Jim "Big Daddy" Walker, and Eddie Heywood passed through before Love broke up this group in 1935. He later formed other bands, including the all-girl Darlings of Rhythm in the 1940s. Love is seated with saxophone at far left, next to the piano. *Kansas City Jazz Museum, Clarence Love Collection.*

65

P̶AUL Banks's Orchestra, from the Kansas side, was a late twenties rival of Moten and Lee. Banks is at the piano in this 1926 picture, with Ed Lewis on trumpet and Jasper "Jap" Allen on tuba. Allen would later lead his own band, and Lewis would be part of the driving brass section in Count Basie's 1930s big band. *Kansas City Jazz Museum, John Baker Collection.*

Kansas City Jazz Museum, Irene Marcus Collection.

Kansas City Jazz Museum, Irene Marcus Collection.

JAP ALLEN'S COTTON CLUB ORCHESTRA

J̶A̶P̶ Allen's orchestra, c.1930. Allen, a Moten contemporary, didn't keep this group together long, but it had some stars: Ben Webster, seated at left, next to pianist Clyde Hart, and, second from right, reedman Booker T. Pittman, who made a name in Europe in the 1930s. *Kansas City Museum, Goin' To Kansas City Collection, Duncan Scheidt.*

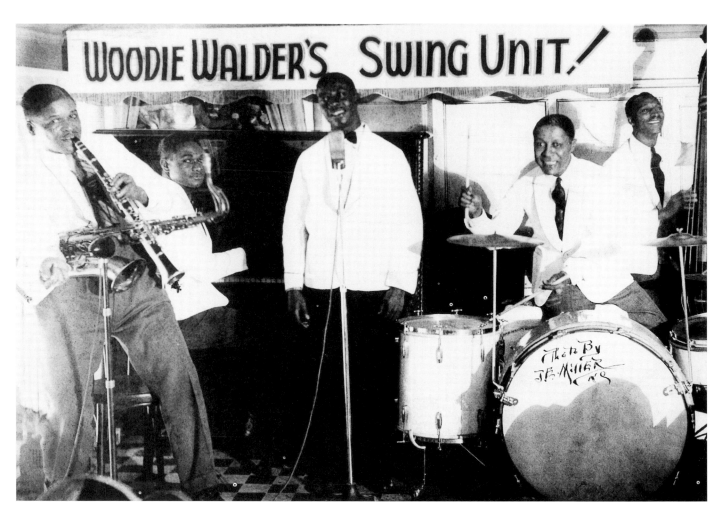

WOODIE Walder's Swing Unit, 1938. Walder and his brother Herman are the stalwart heroes of Kansas City jazz, playing in bands from the 1920s to the 1960s, including the famous Vine Street Varieties broadcasts from the Lincoln Theater in the 1940s. From left: Woodie Walder, reeds; Elbert "Coots" Dye, piano; Bill Terry, vocals; Baby Lovett, drums; Jack Johnson, bass. *Kansas City Jazz Museum, Mattie Story Collection.*

Kansas City Jazz Museum.

THAMON Hayes's band, Fairyland Park, c.1932. This group, cast off in 1931 from Moten's band, bested Moten in the annual Battle of the Bands and took over the coveted summer engagement at Fairyland. From left: Ed Lewis, Baby Lovett, Jesse Stone, Richard Smith, Herman Walder, Thamon Hayes, Vic Dickenson, Woodie Walder, Harlan Leonard, Booker T. Washington, Vernon Page. *Kansas City Museum, Goin' To Kansas City Collection, Charles Goodwin.*

L AURENCE Keyes Orchestra, Lincoln Hall. A version of this band, the Deans of Swing, featured Charlie Parker, then a Lincoln High student, and a young Franz Bruce. The young man who looks like Parker, third sax from left, is Junior Williams. Lincoln Hall was on the third floor of the Lincoln office building at the southeast corner of 18th and Vine. *The Kansas City Call.*

CHAUNCEY Downs and his Rinkey Dinks. Downs went head-to-head with Lee and Moten in 1920s and early 1930s
contests; he was also the unfortunate bandleader on stage when the Fairyland Park pavilion burned to the ground; the fire
had started under the piano. Downs later owned a KC dance hall at 18th and Prospect and played dances through the 1940s.
From left: J. C. Williams, Alex Ashby, Edward Lowery, Ira Jones, Herbert Cranshaw, Elmer Payne, Downs, Harold Walker, Iola
Burton, Lilliam Brown, Lucullus McClellan, Herbert Ashby. *Kansas City Jazz Museum, Claude Page Collection.*

TOMMY Douglas and his orchestra, c.1938. Douglas, a well-respected saxophone player, led large groups from 1930 to
1942, then small combos. Shown here in Fergus Falls, Minncsota, Douglas advertised as "The finest and fastest colored band
on the road." *Kansas City Jazz Museum, John Baker Collection.*

DAVE Lewis's Jazz Boys, Troost Dancing Academy, 15th and Troost, 1922. As early as 1918, Lewis's Famous Colored Jazz Band played at Miss McCue's Dancing School, where white students paid 50 cents a lesson to learn the Charleston and the Black Bottom. From left: Leroy Maxey, DePriest Wheeler, Bill Story, Lawrence Denton, Dude Knox, Roland Bruce, and Dave Lewis. Walter Page started his career sitting in with this group.
Kansas City Jazz Museum, Irene Marcus Collection.

ℬABY Lovett Orchestra, probably at the Chestnut Inn, c.1940. Elbert "Coots" Dye, piano; Ernie Henderson, vocals; Gene Carter, saxophone; Samuel "Baby" Lovett, drums; Jimmy Hill, guitar. Lovett wrote the book on KC jazz drumming, playing with George E. Lee, at the Sunset with Pete Johnson and Joe Turner, with Thamon Hayes's KC Rockets, and for many years with Julia Lee. *Kansas City Jazz Museum, Mattie Story Collection.*

Kansas City Jazz Museum, Emily Vaughn Collection.

THE Five Aces, c.1950. From left: Sonny Kenner, guitar; Larry Cummings (Luqman Hamza), piano; Oscar "Lucky" Wesley, bass; Eddie Saunders, saxophone; Rico Kent, guitar. Formed just after World War II, this group was popular at private dances and parties. *The Kansas City Call.*

JAMES Gadson, Cornealious "Fess" Hill, and Herman Walder in a small combo that became the typical small-group format in the early 1950s. Note Fess's piano "stool." *The Kansas City Call.*

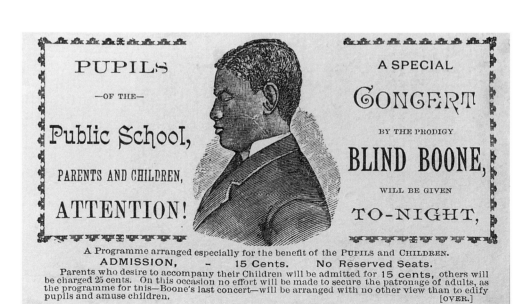

R EEDMAN Ben Kynard, straight out of high school in 1938, was a featured player in many KC groups; by 1949, he was a soloist in Lionel Hampton's orchestra. This photo is back in Kansas City. From left: Wini Brown, Alfred Bartee, Madeline Green, Kynard, Charlie Harris. *The Kansas City Call.*

JIMMIE Keith Combo, Jockey Club, c.1950. From left: Keith, tenor sax; Arthur Mitchell (known to all as "Bonesky"), trombone; Emmett Finney, trumpet; bongo player is unidentified. Keith, well respected as a musician and a gentleman, played in Harlan Leonard's Rockets before leading his own groups. *The Kansas City Call.*

THE Scamps, c.1949. Clockwise from top left: James Whitcomb, Torrence Griffin, Earl Robinson, Wyatt Griffin; Rudy Massengale in center. Formed after World War II, the Scamps, through death and personnel changes, are still performing. And their swinging style still typifies the best of the small-group KC sound. *The Kansas City Call.*

FRANK Miller band at Lincoln Hall, early 1950s. Miller, a pianist, is onstage left of drummer. Stewart Watson, with trumpet at right, later led a group that played many dances. Well into the fifties and early sixties, young new bands sprang up constantly, though the glory days were long gone. *The Kansas City Call.*

From the Kansas side, Charlie Green's band boasted, from left, Henry Hoard, Celester White, Hubert Daniels, Jack Lewis, Green, Theodore Swain, and John Henderson. White would lead many local bands himself in the late forties and fifties. *The Kansas City Call.*

Kansas City Jazz Museum,
Claude Page Collection.

*C*OON-SANDERS Nighthawks, c.1928. Carleton Coon and Joe Sanders led a society dance band, wildly popular in the Midwest through broadcasts, from the Muehlebach Hotel's Plantation Room, on radio station WDAF. Not strictly a jazz band, the Nighthawks recorded and toured extensively. *Kansas City Jazz Museum, Goin' To Kansas City Collection, John Coon.*

Matinee Tomorrow—2:30

RUTH BROWN

Magnificent Blues Singer

with

BILLY CLARK'S ORCHESTRA

EVENING SHOWS 9—11—12:30
Drive to the Door—
Attendant Will Park Your Car!

ORCHID ROOM

1519 East 12th   BA. 1-5157

Kansas City Jazz Museum.

C LAUDE Williams Combo. After playing with a Who's Who of early Kansas City jazz (Andy Kirk, George Lee, Count Basie, Jay McShann), Williams has continued, through the 1990s, as an exceptional player of guitar and violin, including a 1998 White House performance. *Kansas City Jazz Museum.*

$\mathcal{O}$LIVER Todd and his Hottentots, College Inn, 1946. From left: Raymond Ice, Granville Harris, Cleophus Berry, Todd, Pete McShann, Roy Johnson, George Salisbury. With a large terraced dance floor, the College Inn was a swank nightclub downtown. Note the jukebox on the bandstand. *Kansas City Jazz Museum, Oliver Todd Collection.*

Kansas City Jazz Museum.

THE Four Tons of Rhythm, c.1949. From left: Walter Scott, B. C. Kynard, Clint Weaver, Jim "Big Daddy" Walker. A popular rhythm group in the fifties, the Four Tons were deep in experience: Weaver and Walker had played for George E. Lee and Clarence Love, respectively, and Kynard with Clarence Love, among many others. *The Kansas City Call.*

*B*OB Wilson's band. From left: Wilson, Oscar "Lucky" Wesley, Franz Bruce, Claiborne "Frog" Graves, and Paul Gunther.
Wilson played clubs and dances locally into the 1960s. *Kansas City Jazz Museum, Ben Kynard Collection.*

HAVE YOU GOT IT?   YOU HAVE!!
Well Yes! Its at LINCOLN 18th & Vine
HALL
Hear Rev. Bausley preach to you
JITTERBUGS
October 28, 1938.   8;30 uutil 1 o'clock
Admission 25c
The DON RENOS SOCIAL CLUB Kansas City, Mo.

IDA MAE'S TICKETS 100 40C   200 75C   1516 E. 19TH ST.

Kansas City Jazz Museum,
Irene Marcus Collection.

THE Four Tons of Rhythm, c.1955. This later version of the group featured Walter Scott and Lucky Enois on guitar, Claiborne "Frog" Graves on tenor sax, and Clint Weaver on bass. *The Kansas City Call.*

DOROTHY Houston had a remarkable jazz heritage: Her father, Clarence Davis, was a KC trumpeter who later played with Fletcher Henderson, and her mother, Tiny Davis, played with the International Sweethearts of Rhythm. *The Kansas City Call.*

THROUGH his combos and big bands from the forties to the nineties, as well as his teaching, Eddie Baker kept the Kansas City jazz tradition alive. (Opposite page.) *The Kansas City Call.*

Gene Carter. Carter had been playing around town for over ten years when he got a steady date to play the Orchid Room on 12th Street. Nightly, audiences of the 1950s would ask Carter to solo on "Danny Boy," which is still associated with him in Kansas City. *The Kansas City Call.*

L. C. "Speedy" Huggins was a tap dancer, singer, and drummer. He performed from the 1940s into the 1990s and was immensely popular well into his eighties. (Opposite page.) *The Kansas City Call.*

Earl Grant, c.1955. Grant, a longtime KC resident, played many 12th Street clubs in the fifties before signing with Decca Records in 1958, scoring a hit with "The End," and making a career as an "easy listening" pianist and organist. *The Kansas City Call.*

LINCOLN Theater Orchestra, c.1928. From the twenties to the forties, the Lincoln, at 18th and Lydia, hosted vaudeville, touring acts, and local bands as well as movies. When this picture was taken, the leader was James Scott, the ragtime composer and pianist. *Kansas City Jazz Museum, Irene Marcus Collection.*

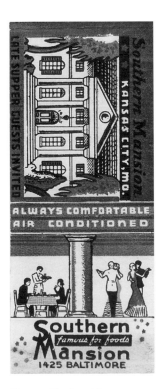

Kansas City Jazz Museum.

LINCOLN Theater staff, c.1928. Composer James Scott and saxophonist Lawrence Denton are ninth and tenth from left. *Kansas City Jazz Museum, Irene Marcus Collection.*

Kansas City Jazz Museum,
Mattie Story Collection.

94

E BLON Theater orchestra, c.1925. Homer "Jap" Eblon opened his theater at 1822 Vine in 1925. The theater band included, from left, drummer Baby Lovett; Homer Franklin, trombone; Eppi Jackson, bass horn; Walter Brown, trumpet; Goopy Taylor, leader and violin; pianist (and ragtime composer) James Scott; and Chick Irvin, saxophone. In just a few years, William Basie would accompany pictures at the Eblon as his first regular job in Kansas City.

Kansas City Jazz Museum, John Baker Collection.

IN the early 1900s, carnivals and minstrel shows were the first steps to the big time: vaudeville. In 1916, twenty-three-year-old Lawrence Denton (third from left) made $12 a week with the Coleman Brothers Circus. The twenty-five-car show played to integrated audiences in the North and West, all in small towns. *Kansas City Jazz Museum, Irene Marcus Collection.*

BY 1918, Lawrence Denton (third from right) had joined Siebrand Bros. Shows and was making $15 a week playing with the carnival band. *Kansas City Jazz Museum, Irene Marcus Collection.*

WHEN Jean Bedini's Peek-A-Boo Revue played the Gayety Theater in downtown Kansas City c.1922, the orchestra (grouped at left) could play in the theater but could not have attended the performance. Reed player Lawrence Denton is fourth from left in this photo of the Bedini company. *Kansas City Jazz Museum, Irene Marcus Collection.*

IN 1938, jazz was everywhere in Kansas City. Minnie Crosthwaite (at left), auxiliary president, made sure Christmas Eve was jazzy for these young Wheatley Hospital patients. At rear is the WPA Swing Orchestra. *The Kansas City Call.*

IN Kansas City, jazz and baseball naturally went together. This photo, c.1938, was taken at a Monarchs game. Starting at center, this saxophone section includes Cleophus Berry, Curtyse Foster, Freddie Culliver, Herman and Woodie Walder, and Franz Bruce. *The Kansas City Call.*

LAWRENCE Denton, c.1965. Denton, who began at age eighteen, was still playing in his eighties. At the time of this photo, he was leading a band of older musicians, playing at retirement homes for appreciative audiences. (Opposite page.) *Kansas City Jazz Museum, Irene Marcus Collection.*

N the 1930s, the Works Progress Administration (WPA) sponsored bands and cultural projects across the country, including Kansas City. This group played concerts and benefits, such as this show for the Kansas City Boys Orphan Home in 1938.
Kansas City Jazz Museum, Irene Marcus Collection.

T<small>HE</small> Musicians' Protective Union, Local 627, fields a band in the 1939 NAACP parade. Ernie Williams can be seen directing the group, and Herman Walder, top left, on saxophone. *Kansas City Jazz Museum, Mabel Jones Collection.*

Kansas City Jazz Museum.

E LKS Band, 1928.
Marching bands were
an important part of a musician's development, but they
were also a source of community pride and ritual for
organized social groups and
societies. The Elks organized
parades through the community through the 1950s and
traveled to competitions
nationally. In picture at right
the Elks are shown at a
Chicago contest.
*Kansas City Jazz Museum,
Irene Marcus Collection.*

TO·NIGHT

—AT THE—

PUPILS' AND CHILDREN'S

SPECIAL CONCERT,

BOONE WILL PLAY:

"Nearer My God to Thee," with his variations,
"Beulah Land," with his variations,
Mocking Bird,
Home, Sweet Home,
Brown's Jubilee March,

and a number of common, national and sacred airs. Will also sing a few sacred or sentimental songs, and a goodly number of Negro Camp-meeting, Plantation, and Comic songs. He will imitate on his piano the fife and drum, calliope, banjo, guitar, music-box, the country fiddler, and cars, and will make fun for the boys with his mouth-organ. Will play two pieces at one time; will play two instruments at one time. He will conclude with his own grand and thrilling Cyclone Imitation.

Parents should bear in mind that there has never been but two such musical "freaks of nature," and that Boone's audiences everywhere are made up of the cultured and intelligent, and that this may be the last chance for their children to hear either of these blind colored musical wonders, and since the programme is arranged to entertain and also make fun for pupils and children, and the price put at 15 cents, and since an entertainment of this character has no objectionable features, we trust that every pupil and child in the city will avail himself of this opportunity to attend this

SPECIAL CONCERT.

B̶UNNIE "Bumps" Love was popular in the fifties as a single and with small groups. Swinging ballads were Bumps's style. *The Kansas City Call.*

E VELYN Twine is remembered as a ballad and blues singer with Bob Wilson's band in the forties and fifties.
The Kansas City Call.

Myra Taylor is remembered for her fine work as a vocalist with Harlan Leonard's Rockets in 1940–41, and her national R & B hit, "The Spider and the Fly." Taylor, niece of blues singer Ada Brown, toured internationally into the 1970s.
The Kansas City Call.

CHARLOTTE Mansfield was a popular headliner in town, playing as a single and with three pieces; she recorded briefly with Capitol Records. *Kansas City Jazz Museum, Oliver Todd Collection.*

JOSEPHINE Byrd was a blues and ballad singer in the Ethel Waters tradition. She sang in clubs in town and was popular in roadhouses outside the city limits. *The Kansas City Call.*

Margaret "Countess" Johnson is remembered fondly as a pianist to rival Kansas City's best. Tragically, she died young. Johnson began her career playing piano in Mother Sutton's church, but by the late 1930s she was jamming in clubs and often sat in for Mary Lou Williams with the Clouds of Joy. She recorded four sides in 1938, with Billie Holiday and some Basie regulars. *Kansas City Jazz Museum, Bud Taylor Collection.*

IRENE McLaurian was a multitalented pianist, singer, and dancer. She often sang with Bob Wilson's band, and she operated a dance school for a number of years. In this 1945 session at the Flamingo Club at 39th and Main, she is surrounded by Cleophus Berry, bass; Oliver Todd, trumpet; and Ben Webster, tenor saxophone. *Kansas City Jazz Museum, Oliver Todd Collection.*

*B*IG Joe Turner, the nonpareil blues shouter, began singing in Kansas City joints on Independence Avenue as a teenager, drawing a mustache on his upper lip in an attempt to look older. By the early 1930s, he was a singing bartender at the Sunset Crystal Palace on 12th Street. "I don't think I'll ever forget the thrill," said Mary Lou Williams, "of listening to Big Joe Turner, shouting and sending everybody, night after night, while mixing drinks." Turner's natural exuberance was matched by the driving piano of Pete Johnson, his longtime partner. Turner and Johnson were wildly successful in New York, after 1939. In the 1950s, Turner began a second career of sorts, as a creator of rock 'n' roll. "This rock 'n' roll is nothin' new," Turner said. "It's the same as I've been singing since 1936, in Kansas City." *Kansas City Jazz Museum, John Baker Collection.*

Bettye Miller, Milt Abel. This duo's smooth sound made them Kansas City's premier small-combo act in the fifties and sixties. Although they toured little, they were a regional attraction and they were the city's most visible jazz asset of that time. *Kansas City Museum, Goin' To Kansas City Collection and Mutual Musicians Foundation.*

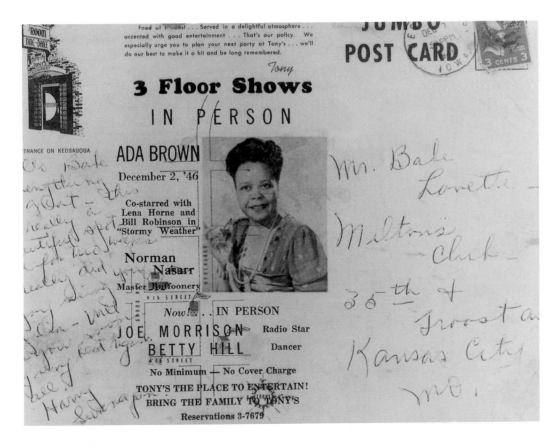

ADA Brown with Harry Swanagan. Brown was a remarkable talent, performing from 1921 (in the Lincoln Theater pit) until she retired in 1948. She had toured nationally as a blues singer by the time she recorded "Break o' Day Blues" with Bennie Moten's orchestra in 1923. She continued to tour with pianist Harry Swanagan and also appeared with Fats Waller in the 1943 film *Stormy Weather*. Brown was a cousin of ragtime composer James Scott and an aunt of singer Myra Taylor. *Kansas City Jazz Museum, Mattie Story Collection.*

PEPPER Neely was a popular balladeer in the forties and fifties, often singing with altoist Walter Knight's group. The mention of Neely's name to Kansas Citians over sixty can trigger a rendition of "In the Chapel in the Moonlight." *The Kansas City Call.*

MARSHALL "Garbage" Rogers. This Chicago comedian was a Kansas City favorite. Comedians, dancers, and other novelty acts were part of a complete floor show at many clubs. (Opposite page.) *The Kansas City Call.*

115

Sleepy's Trio, c.1942. Mary Lou Williams compared Edward "Sleepy" Hickcox favorably with Art Tatum; according to Oliver Todd, "That guy played a whole lot of piano." Hickcox played bop with Charlie Parker at Tootie's Mayfair; he played with small combos, as in this photo with Oscar Minor and Orville Demoss; and he was Parker's favorite piano player, according to Eddie Saunders. Hickcox never became known outside Kansas City. *The Kansas City Call.*

DAN Blackburn's Municipal Band started as a brass band in 1917, and Blackburn held concerts in Parade Park until 1945. The Sunday shows were a big event, Lawrence Denton remembered. "Sometimes we played for three or four thousand, five thousand people would come out there to hear the band. . . . We played a mixture: ragtime and marches, and classics, waltzes."
Kansas City Jazz Museum, Irene Marcus Collection.

LINCOLN High School Band, 1920. Major N. Clark Smith, director, is at right, rear. This band marched in every patriotic parade held in the city, including the Red Cross and Liberty Bond parades and the parade in support of the proposed Liberty Memorial. The Lincoln band was the Eleventh Regiment Band of the High School Cadets of Kansas City, Missouri. *Kansas City Jazz Museum, Irene Marcus Collection.*

A SELECTED JAZZ BIBLIOGRAPHY

compiled by Leonard Brown

Armstrong, Louis. *Satchmo: My Life in New Orleans*. New York: Prentice Hall, 1954.

Basie, Count. *Good Morning Blues: The Autobiography of Count Basie as Told to Albert Murray*. New York: Random House, 1985.

Dahl, Linda. *Stormy Weather: The Music and Lives of a Century of Jazzwomen*. New York: Pantheon Books, 1984.

DeVeaux, Scott. *Birth of Bebop: A Social Musical History*. Berkeley, Calif.: University of California Press, 1997.

Driggs, Frank. "Kansas City and the Southwest." In *Jazz: New Perspectives on the History of Jazz by Twelve of the World's Jazz Critics and Scholars,* eds. Nat Hentoff and Albert J. McCarthy. New York: Da Capo Press, 1974.

Ellington, Edward Kennedy. *Music Is My Mistress*. New York: Da Capo Press, 1976.

Harrison, Daphne Duval. *Black Pearls: Blues Queens of the 1920s*. New Brunswick, N.J.: Rutgers University Press, 1988.

Jones, Leroi. *Blues People*. New York: Morrow Quill Paperbacks, 1963.

Kofsky, Frank. *Black Nationalism and the Revolution in Music*. New York: Pathfinder Press, 1970.

Leonard, Neil. *Jazz: Myth and Religion*. New York: Oxford University Press, 1987.

Murray, Albert. *Stomping the Blues*. New York: Da Capo Press, 1987.

Pearson, Nathan W., Jr. *Goin' to Kansas City*. Chicago: University of Illinois Press, 1987.

Porter, Lewis, Michael Ullman, and Edward Hazell. *Jazz: From Its Origins to the Present*. Englewood Cliffs, N.J.: Prentice-Hall, 1993.

Schuller, Gunther. *Early Jazz: Its Roots and Musical Development*. New York: Oxford University Press, 1968.

———. *The Swing Era: The Development of Jazz, 1930–1945*. New York: Oxford University Press, 1989.

Shapiro, Nat, and Nat Hentoff eds. *Hear Me Talkin' to Ya: The Story of Jazz As Told by the Man Who Made It*. New York: Dover, 1966.

Sidran, Ben. *Black Talk*. New York: Da Capo Press, 1981.

Southern, Eileen. *The Music of Black Americans: A History*, 2nd ed. New York: W. W. Norton, 1983.

———. *Readings in Black American Music*. New York: W. W. Norton, 1983.

Stearns, Marshall W. *The Story of Jazz*. New York: Oxford University Press, 1970.

Taylor, Arthur. *Notes and Tones*. New York: Perigee Books, 1982.

Taylor, William. *Jazz Piano: History and Development*. Iowa: WCD, 1983.

Tirro, Frank. *Jazz: A History*. 2nd ed. New York: W. W. Norton, 1983.

Walton, Ortiz. *Music: Black, White, and Blue*. New York: William Morrow, 1972.

A SELECTED JAZZ VIDEOGRAPHY

compiled by Leonard Brown

Celebrating Bird: The Triumph of Charlie Parker
Documentary on the life of the legendary Kansas City genius.

Coltrane Legacy
Documentary on the music of John Coltrane.

Good Morning Blues
Hosted by B. B. King, this documentary focuses on the legacy of Mississippi Delta blues and how the music moved north via black migrations.

Hootie's Blues
Documentary on the music of Jay McShann, available through Nebraska Educational Television.

International Sweethearts of Rhythm
Documentary featuring legacy of one of the first all-female jazz bands of the 1930s.

The Last of the Blue Devils
Documentary filmed in Kansas City that focuses on the legacy of the great territory bands.

Machito: A Latin Jazz Legacy
Documentary on the outstanding contributions of Frank Grillo, Mario Banza, and the Afro-Cubans to jazz and salsa.

The Many Faces of Billie Holiday
Excellent documentary on the great blues and jazz singer.

Music on My Mind
Documentary on the legacy of Mary Lou Williams.

My Castle's Rockin'
Documentary on the life and music of Alberta Hunter.

Satchmo: The Story of Louis Armstrong
Documentary featuring the life and music of the first great jazz soloist.

The Songs Are Free
Documentary by Bernice Reagon Johnson highlighting the roles and functions of spirituals in the African American experience.

Swinging the Blues
Documentary on the Count Basie legacy, hosted by Albert Murray.

That Rhythm, Those Blues
Documentary on roles and functions of rhythm and blues in the late 1940s and early 1950s. Features blues greats Ruth Brown and Charles Brown.

Wild Women Don't Have the Blues
Documentary chronicling the great classic African American female blues singers of the early twentieth century.